Brian and Lynne Chatterton bought a hill farm in Umbria in the heart of Italy in 1990. The stone farm house, built originally by monks from a nearby abbey, had been deserted for thirty years and and the olive grove was being reclaimed by the surrounding forest. This is an account of their experiences in restoring their olive grove, planting more trees and discovering the traditional and scientific methods of olive growing and oil pressing.

Before moving to Italy, Brian and Lynne grew grapes, and farmed cereals and sheep in the Barossa Valley in South Australia as well as making red wine and a unique white port. Brian was Minister of Agriculture in the Dunstan Government during the 1970's and Lynne was Rural Policy Adviser to Don Dunstan. Besides growing olives in the hills of Umbria they now advise on dryland farming in North Africa and West Asia. In between, Lynne is trying to find time to write a book about food.

GW00601966

Also by Brian and Lynne Chatterton:

Sustainable Dryland Farming - Combining farmer innovation and medic pasture in a Mediterranean climate. Cambridge University Press 1996.

Fodders for the Near East: annual medic pastures. Food & Agriculture Organisation of the United Nations. Rome 1989.

Why grow medic?
Establishing a medic pasture.
Grazing management and the seed reserve.
Cereals and medic in rotation.
Food & Agriculture Organisation of the United Nations. Rome 1988.

Home Wine-making. Rigby, Adelaide 1972.

DISCOVERING OIL

TALES FROM AN OLIVE GROVE IN UMBRIA

by

Brian and Lynne Chatterton

PULCINI PRESS

Castel di Fiori & Renwick

First published 1999 by Pulcini Press,
4 Anglesea St, Renwick, N.Z.
Head Office: Castel di Fiori,
05010 Montegabbione (TR) ITALIA.

Distributors in New Zealand:

Hunters Wines (NZ) Ltd.
P.O. Box 839,
Blenheim, N.Z.
Email: hunters@voyager.co.nz

Distributors in Australia:

Bottega Rotolo
7-9 Osmond Terrace
Norwood 5067
AUSTRALIA
Email: bottega_rot@picknowl.com.au

Photos: Florita Botts

Printed and bound in New Zealand by:

Blenheim Print
12 Boyce Street,
Blenheim, NZ

ISBN 0-473-06289-5

CONTENTS

Chapter 1

OLIVES IN THE UMBRIAN LANDSCAPE

A brief history of olive oil production in Central Italy

Olives have been cultivated for thousands of years in the Mediterranean region and there are indications that they were grown in Umbria by the Etruscans who farmed the rich valley land around 600 BC. It is likely that the more primitive Umbri tribes who were in the high hill country also grew olives from very early times.

Mediaeval documents reveal that olives in Umbria and Tuscany were planted only in small numbers until the last century. Farm records show there were two or three trees here and half a dozen there on individual holdings. The production of oil was low and was a small part of the produce due from the share farmer to the landowner. The share farmer often sold his portion for a little cash in order to buy salt or shoes. Most peasant families used lard from their pig for cooking. Oil was too expensive to use daily. Their diet largely depended on wheat, ground into flour and made into bread and pasta. This, with home made and conserved tomato sauce, supplemented by vegetables grown in their "orto", and fruit and funghi from the forest provided most meals. A ewe provided milk for cheese and occasionally pigeons (that roosted in baskets in the loggia) were put in the pot. Little meat was available and when the pig or a sheep was slaughtered it provided festive meals and winter stores.

While a great deal of farming in Europe has been modernised, mechanised and subsidised, olive growing remains largely a family concern using the same criteria that began centuries ago.

Our village provides a tiny example of this. One of our neighbors owns most of the best farming land in the valley. The historical continuity of farming on this land is illustrated by the fact that he benefits today from drainage carried out over 800 years ago. His fields in those days were swamp land flooded by the runoff from the surrounding hills until they were cleverly drained by mediaeval monks through a system of interception ditches that led the water along the side of the hill into the creeks before it spread over the low lying fields. The concept of intercepting the spate from the surrounding hills began elsewhere even before our monks carried out this work. The Etruscans, centuries before, initiated this sort of drainage on the larger valley systems of the Tiber and Chiani rivers. These valleys are now the richest and most productive land in Umbria. Farmers who own land in these valleys grow a variety of cereals - sometimes wheat and maize in the same year with irrigation. Sunflowers, tobacco and sugar beet are also grown but our neighbor confines himself to cereals with the occasional forage crop for hay. He also has a patch of vines. In spite of the interception drainage he does not grow olives in this valley. His olives are planted on the slopes that are steep and stony. Tradition, now confirmed by science, dictates that this is the best olive land and he agrees.

There is a much greater production of olives and oil in the south of Italy than in the Centre and north of Italy and today in the South there are trees, now protected as national monuments, that are hundreds of years old. On a horticultural study trip around Caserta, on the rich alluvial plains near Naples, we found one orchardist who had a magnificent tree in his front garden. It must have been some two or three hundred years old and the trunk had a diameter of nearly a metre. The top canopy was sparse after three centuries of hard pruning, but it still produced olives. We congratulated him on his good fortune in having such a tree so well placed in the centre of the garden but, much to our surprise, he told us he had moved it to his new house from another part of his farm because he was so fond of it.

Individual trees in our region are not enormously old because of the severe frosts that occur here every thirty or so years. There are some trees that are said to be a hundred years old or more on the shores and islands of lake Trasimeno where the frost is moderated by the water. If you are rich it is possible to buy hundred-year-old trees in plastic pots from our local plant and tree nursery. They sell for between two and five thousand dollars each. It is sobering to remember that the trees in the parks in Adelaide, South Australia, are probably older than most of the currently productive olives in Umbria and Tuscany.

While the origins of the olive tree are ancient, the commercial oil industry is not. Towards the end of the 19th century there was an expansion in wine and olive production due to a shakeup of the large landholdings. The Church sold up a lot of its land in Umbria and the Risorgimento that resulted in the unification of Italy created many new fortunes and many new titles. The new landholders wanted to make their new properties pay and the emergence at about the same time of a relatively prosperous middle class in the cities created a profitable market for olive oil. Industrial oil mills capable of producing more oil than was needed for the family or farm were introduced, although many small centres still depended upon traditional presses.

Oil to the people

Between the 20th century wars Mussolini encouraged and reinforced the share farming system because he believed that it contributed to social stability in the countryside. He made it difficult for share farmers - even if they could scrape together the funds - to buy their farms. The historically exploitative nature of the system had sent many share farmers into the radical movements of Communism and anarchism and this reinforcement caused many more to join. The contadini (share farmers) made up the rural backbone of the Communist Party and remained so even when, after the second world war, the plight of the farmer improved. Umbria, Tuscany, Emilia Romagna and the Marche are still the "Red Centre" of Italy to this day and return a solid block of Left members to the national parliament.

With the demise of Mussolini the share farming system fragmented. Communist-led farm workers and share farmers occupied many large estates. This shamed the post-war government into some land reform and forced changes to the law. In general, the land reform program was not a success due in part to its origin in political opportunism, and in part to the economic ineptitude and paternalistic control exercised by the government administration charged with the implementation of the reforms.

The reform program also foundered on the determination of many farm workers and share farmers to leave agriculture altogether. They were fed up with the poverty, the grind, and the desperately hard work on farms and when they were offered small pieces of land under the new land reform program this attempt to keep them on the land held no attraction for them. Opportunities were open to them to go to the Northern cities to work in newly built industrial plants, to go to Switzerland and other Northern European countries to work on building sites, in hotels, in trades - all of which paid them wages in cash in quantities they had never before seen in their lives.

Land reform, after nearly a century of holding out hope to the rural poor, had come too late. Share farmers voted with their feet and left for greener fields in their hundreds of thousands. They left behind a landscape that rapidly fossilised into one of deserted farmhouses and abandoned farmland.

Without an abundant supply of cheap labour land owners simply neglected their land. In Australia extensive grazing with sheep is always an option when all other enterprises fail but in Umbria livestock needed shepherds to guard and care for them and they had all gone to find better lives. The fields were too small for mechanised cereal farming and most of the land was left to the encroaching forest.

The radical legal changes that had finally given rights to the share farmers and rural workers after a century of dithering not only came too late but imposed conditions on land use that stifled any more equitable agreement between the landholder and the remaining contadini. The laws of tenancy which had allowed the landowners to exploit the share farmer were now radically skewed in favor of the tenant. If a tenant works the land for 10 consecutive years he is entitled to petition the court to award him outright ownership of it or the right to buy it at a nominal sum. Under these conditions no landowner dared rent his land on a long term tenancy and preferred to leave it unused rather than risk losing his title to it. Today the agrarian question has fallen off the political agenda and modernisation of the tenancy laws is unlikely. Politicians now discuss flexible labour markets not flexible land use.

While the new laws put an end to much farming it did not mean that olive growing died out. The olives, unlike the vines, survived in the abandoned landscape with little attention and many were harvested by local families on informal shares with the land owner. There were still some share farmers who did take advantage of the right to buy land and, in Umbria particularly, many became small landholders and established their farms with mixed crops. They grow fruit, vines and olives, keep a few sheep, a pig or two and some dairy cows. Some are dependent upon off-farm work and rely on their wives to do the daily farm work, taking their factory holidays at times of seasonal demand. Most government workers (roads, railways, post offices and so on) work only half the day at fairly low wages to qualify for their early pensions and so are able to contribute significant labour to their own enterprises.

Guest workers who returned to their place of birth when they retired came back with sufficient money to buy a parcel of land and build a house on it. Olives and vines were particularly attractive to them because not only could they produce enough oil and wine for their immediate family, but they could barter the surplus with other family members who would trade skills or labour. Any further surplus could be sold to the local mill for welcome cash. Many continue to work elsewhere, but return during the long summer break and help the brother or cousin who manages the farm to harvest and process the wine and later to collect the oil from the mill and share it out.

As always historical catastrophes favor profiteers, and there were those who made fortunes out of either the war or its aftermath. They were keen to establish gentry connections and they bought country estates, restored the farmhouses for summer residences, employed a local farmer to do the heavy work and delighted in wine and oil of their own provenance.

In our village, the "padrone" who owned most of the land around the village obviously believed that things would continue as they had done before the war as he built an extra wing onto our house in 1950. For a while three families lived on our farm of seven hectares. The men worked for the padrone and the adjoining forest provided grazing and forage for animals and funghi and berries for the kitchen and firewood for the stoves. The local government also believed that life would continue as before as they built a school for the considerable population of village children at about the same time. Fifteen years later our farm was abandoned, the school was closed and the few children who remained were bussed to the larger village nearby. The population of 350 for the village and surrounding farms in the 1950's has crashed to 10 today.

One sees thousands and thousands of hectares of abandoned farm land with their deserted farm houses throughout Umbria. Where they have been restored it is usually foreigners, such as ourselves, who have bought them to use as summer houses and, more rarely, to live in permanently. Italians from the large cities have now joined this trend set by the foreigners. It provides local employment and supports local shops and artisans, and best of all, nearly every one of the newcomers plants olives for their own olive oil.

Stones, stones and more stones and olives

Stones dominated the life of the share farmer in the hills. They made his life a misery. He picked them out of the fields, carted them into heaps and then when the heaps took up too much room, turned them into dry stone walls. The attractive dry stone walls that form the terraces of the abandoned hill farms are not retaining walls for deep and fertile soil but controlled stone heaps. We found this out the hard way when we planted half a dozen walnut and chestnut trees in a small terraced field behind our house. Most of the holes we dug hit sheet rock but when we dug near the walls in the expectation of finding a good depth of soil we found only loose stones. On our farm the lay brothers from the abbey at the bottom of the hill (who had established our little farm and built our original house), had picked up the stones off the hillside with a sledge drawn by oxen, put them in a heap and then built a wall below the heap to prevent the stones rolling down to the field below. A little soil was scraped onto the loose stones but the walls did little to improve fertility. The best that can be said was that they helped avoid erosion when the heavy rainstorms poured down the steep hillsides. . As farmers abandoned marginal cereal production on their small hill farms, many of these stony fields were planted to olive trees.

Today the walls are continually falling down but there is no one interested in repairing them and occasionally contractors buy sections of them and cart them off as good clean fill. It is hard to blame the farmer for this destruction of the landscape. Having spent a lifetime fighting to control the stones he must be delighted when someone offers to pay to take them away completely. In a few more decades the dry stone walls that form such an important part of the landscape will no longer be neat lines across the hillsides but tumbled heaps of stones with a few patches of wall still standing.

We began by repairing some of the fallen walls in our fields, but the work has now become an annual winter event. Once the vipers that lurk in stone heaps have gone to bed, the cement mixer and the stone carter come out and work begins. We found that we could not have a garden unless we tamed the erosion and got some soil in, so building new dry stone walls (backed by concrete for security) provided us with terraces and garden beds and, we think, a rather charming garden.

The steep slopes and stony fields that surround us are traditional olive country. In fact the old Italian saying is that olives need the five S's. They are

silenzio, siccita, solitudine, sole e sassi.

It is just possible to translate them into English keeping the five S's. They become

silence, stress (water stress or drought), solitude, sun and *stones.*

The "silence" and the "solitude" are part of the poetic aura surrounding the growing of olives but the other three "S's" are still considered important contributors to quality olive oil production.

The forest

Above the olive zone is the even steeper and more stony land where the oak forests grow. Rural depopulation has changed these forests too. Fifty years ago they were full of huge old trees and underneath the glades were clear. The trees were harvested now and then for roof beams and railway sleepers. Underneath them farmers grazed their sheep on poor quality pasture and in the autumn pigs foraged for acorns.

Railway sleepers and roof beams are now made from reinforced concrete and the forest is cut every fifteen years for boutique firewood. We call it "boutique" firewood because the common fuel for cooking and heating in Italy today is Algerian natural gas piped across Tunisia and under the sea to Sicily but restaurants like to advertise their wood fired ovens for pizze and chic apartments in Rome have an ornamental open fire and forest trees provide the wood for these gestures to rusticity. Our neighbor has a large area of forest surrounding his arable land and harvests the firewood during the winter after the cereal crops have been sown and before pruning the vines and olives. The result of the cutting has been that the forests are now overgrown with bush and shrubs and are largely dense thickets of regrowth.

The forests are mostly privately owned but the community has certain rights of access and harvesting. Italy did not take part in the transformation of land into a personal commodity which took place in Britain in the 18th and 19th centuries. This excluded all community rights from the land and transferred them to the private owner. This concept of ownership was transferred to Australia and New Zealand where it remained in force until it was challenged by Aboriginal and Maori claims for land rights.

In Italy many community rights over privately owned land remain today. The forests are harvested for firewood by contractors working for the owners or sometimes by the owners themselves. When the last of the saleable wood has been carted out with the mule teams local residents can "glean" the forest for any wood left. This is mostly the light material - the fasce - which are bundled up, stacked on the roof of the trusty old Fiat 500 and taken home to fuel the pizza oven.

Populations of wild boar in the forest remain targets for hunters who exercise community rights. There is some hunting in late autumn for birds such as pheasant but most of the effort goes into hunting the boar. Italians have had hunting rights over land for centuries. By contrast many of Australia's first migrants were British farm workers who were transported for life for poaching game on private land in the last century.

Fortunately for those of us who live in the forest there are proscribed seasons for hunters and it is forbidden outside these declared periods. Hunters need a government permit but not the owners' permission. Hunting today is usually carried out by well organised groups who live in the larger towns and cities and who have an incredible amount of fire power and packs of dogs to flush out the pigs. There is pressure to ban or manage hunting for conservation reasons but so far attempts to change the law by referendum have failed. No one is even considering calling for the private ownership of hunting rights.

Besides the wild boar there are large numbers of porcupine which were hunted and eaten as a delicacy in the past. They are now protected but at times we wish they were not. We often see them at night. They are a most spectacular sight when they are caught in the car headlights with their spines erect. They look like huge tropical fish. They are not the favorite animal of those who live here. We, and all our neighbors, suffer from their extraordinarily destructive habits. They ravage potato crops, tomato plants and bulbs and eat off the new broad beans just before we are set to enjoy the harvest. They have no fear and rampage through our garden at night digging for bulbs and tubers. Tulips are their favorite. They dig in open beds and turn large pots over in their foraging. Their numbers have increased in the ten years we have lived here, and they have completely destroyed many existing drifts of sky blue iris that formerly covered the slopes with heavenly blue in the spring time.

Community rights also exist to walk the old trails through countryside and forest. Woe betide anyone who attempts to "privatise" these trails - sabotage and court cases rapidly reverse the situation and the trails remain open to all. The dense regrowth in parts of the forest today makes walking these traditional trails difficult but it does provides protection for the nests of the nightingales which provide us with beautiful harmonies in spring and early summer. They are a contrast to monotonous call of the cuckoos that also inhabit the forest. Pheasants and other birds, including the migratory hoopoo, are protected by this thick bush and add to the interest of those who value bird life. The various authorities concerned with the forests periodically clean up the old trails and put blaze marks on trees so that those who wish can enjoy them and we often enjoy a good tramp when the weather is cool and there is a bit of time to spare.

The community right to harvest mushrooms has also been preserved. As soon as spring and autumn rains fall our neighbors climb our hill and range over the nearby fields with knives and baskets at the ready searching for the range of mushrooms, the most famous of which is the funghi porcini, that they are passionate about. The forests are also home to the tartufo - the truffle as the French call it - and these are harvested by professional hunters with trained dogs. Most only hunt part time as the tartufo emits the strongest perfume at dawn. As it gets warmer the smell disperses and the dogs find it harder to pick it up. The hunters go into the forest at 5 am for a couple of hours and then go on to work in the nearby towns or as service station attendants on the autostrada. Sales of tartufo provide a useful additional income once they have paid out $800 for the training of the dog and $400 for the government permit. One of the tartufo hunters who calls on us every few months to have a good gossip is 84 years old and has been living off tartufo sales most of his life. He travels to other parts of Umbria and Tuscany in search of the white tartufo which is worth double the poor grade black tartufo with a grey centre that is found in our forest. He also goes to the forests of the Appenine mountain chain behind Assisi to hunt for the even more valuable black tartufo with a black centre. While there is no obligation to inform or pay the landowner for the tartufi we find that many of the hunters who take tartufi from our land give us one or two as a token.

The value of olives to Italian families can be illustrated by the fact that although all these hunters and walkers have the right to approach within one hundred metres of a house to pursue their quarry, they are forbidden to enter an olive grove. This may well be to protect two of the five "S's" sacred to olive growing - those of "solitude" and "silence".

Olive growing today

There is a conflict today over where best to grow olives for quality oil. The olive oil *afficionado* drools over the taste of the oil from the high country and the steep stony land from where we get the strongest flavored Umbrian oils. Over 90% of the olives are grown in hill and mountain country. However, yields are low and erratic.

Those who emphasise farm economics and management favor using better land, for example land formerly used for cereal production, because the deeper soil produces higher yields and trees come into production quicker.

Commercial growers are adopting this latter advice and abandoning the high country although it is still prized by those who grow olives for oil for their own family.

But there are some olive growers with their own *frantoio* (mill) and retail outlet who are having second thoughts. As the market begins to appreciate the quality of oils produced from small olive groves in the high country, they are able, by selling direct to consumers themselves, to get $25 a litre or more for this premium oil, or double the usual wholesale price, and this can make the hill country pay.

Chapter 2

WHAT IS A PREMIUM OIL?

Our first olive trees

The abandoned farmhouse that friends found for us in Umbria stood in the middle of some hectares of equally abandoned land and on part of that land were abandoned olive trees. The pressure of our neighbors upon us to produce our own household olive oil, slowly pushed us into the game. "How can you leave those trees like that?", they asked. People from the larger village nearby said they'd give their eyeteeth to have a few trees and the oil from them - "you'd get enough for yourselves", they would calculate. Some offered to pick the olives for us - fifty/fifty shares as is the custom here. We did this the first year and received one bottle each. The oil was splendid - green, fruity and spicy.

The following spring we decided to act. We really believed that olives would be hassle free and that all we would have to do was to pick the fruit and have it pressed. It didn't turn out quite like that. But, you can't keep a good farmer down and it wasn't long before we began enthusiastically to look for ways to lift yield and reduce physical labour and, as we have always been great cooks, to use more and more of our oil in our kitchen. Our neighbors were pleased at our adoption of "their ways" and bent over backwards to help us learn the local olive lore.

We came to live permanently in Italy in 1990 after selling our farm in the Barossa Valley in South Australia where we had run a thousand sheep, sown and harvested wheat and barley and made wine from a small vineyard. We had no ambition to settle in a town or city and searched high and low through Tuscany and Umbria for a place in the country before settling here. We knew we didn't want to get into sheep rearing again, nor to grow grain, and we certainly weren't going to plant vines and make wine - apart from the never ending spray program necessary to mature grapes here, we were surrounded by good wine makers and their wine was cheap - why make life harder than it is, we told ourselves. But olives took us over. Olives are an integral part of the Mediterranean landscape, they are part of the culture and are surrounded by myths. Even the English, who for many centuries had no time for olives or their oil, used the phrase "holding out an olive branch" that derived from a benevolent myth about olives.

During the years we lived in Barossa Valley in South Australia we found ourselves gradually replacing with olive oil the salted butter and vegetable oil used in those days in Australian cooking. We began by buying fairly ordinary oil from Spain and Greece, and later learnt to value the better oils from Italy. In the 1980's when we were working frequently in North Africa, Rome was our base for acquiring visas and making flight connections to Tunisia, Libya, Morocco and Algeria. As we became more familiar with Roman food we noticed how restaurants had bottles of olive oil on the table and how Italians added this oil to their salads, their cooked vegetables and even their soup. The Romans told us that the oil itself was an essential condiment for these dishes. They valued most of all oil that came from an olive grove that they knew well - a family property or that of a friend.

The characteristics of good oil

We began living in Italy in the late 1980's. We rented part of a country villa in the hills above Frascati and began cooking our own meals. We thought buying tasty olive oil would be easy. The supermarket shelves were groaning with olive oils of every grade and price. We soon found that the label "extravergine" did not guarantee those delicious flavors we enjoyed in restaurants and we realised that we had to learn a lot more about the characteristics of good olive oil.

In the aisles of supermarkets, even in Italy, it is not easy to spot the best oil. Even in the chic boutiques, where elegant bottles, artistic labels and high prices promise much more, we were often disappointed in the contents. We had somehow to get hold of the same oil that the restaurants used.

In 1990 we came here to our long abandoned farm and began to find the answer to our questions and to learn, as olive growers, just what made olive oil taste good.

"Extravergine" (or "Extra Virgin" in English) has become fixed in the minds of many people as the symbol of excellent oil. Celebrity chefs on British TV all say "extra virgine of course" in a hushed tone of reverence whenever they pick up the olive oil bottle. It is the first requirement of quality but it tells you little about the flavor of the oil.

We knew from experience with wine that processing, no matter how good, doesn't determine the taste of the wine. For example, it is possible to make a technically excellent wine from Sultanas but it is classed in the trade as "neutral" as it has no taste. To make a wine full of flavor and bouquet other varieties such as Chardonnay or Sauvignon Blanc are necessary.

The taste test illustrates this. In 1993 we were sent a tiny bottle of boutique extravergine olive oil from Marlborough in New Zealand. The oil in the 200 ml bottle was selling for about $70 a litre. Technically it was top quality. We decided to test it against the Italian oils in a blind tasting. We always had Christmas with our neighbors who collected the whole family of three generations from grand parents to grand children for a traditional lunch. We put a collection of oils into carefully numbered jars. There were two of our own local oils from different years, the New Zealand oil, a premium oil produced from the hills above Assisi, and another excellent oil produced from similar country behind Foligno. We put one of the oils in twice, an old trick we learnt from wine tasting days in the Barossa Valley, to check on the tasters' ability to distinguish the oils.

All the family joined in with great enthusiasm. The first thing we learned was that Italians are passionate about olive oil - much more than they are about wine. They all picked our local oil as the best (at that time we put our olives in with theirs for crushing so our oil was identical) but some members of the family liked the new oil that was a month old and had plenty of bite, while others preferred the milder taste of the oil from the previous season which had softened with age. The oils from Assisi and Foligno ranked a strong second but the New Zealand oil came a poor last. After revealing the scores we tackled them on their downgrading of the New Zealand oil and they all said it was technically fine, there were no off-flavors, but it lacked "bite" or a distinctive flavor.

Following the New Zealand oil to its source

The tasting and the comments intrigued us and we decided to follow the oil trail back to the trees when we visited New Zealand a few years later. We tasted oils at a "frantoio" (olive mill) near Blenheim and in spite of the fact that the trees were mature the oil, to our palates, had little or no flavor. Press reports at the time said how some local oil had been tested in Madrid by the International Olive Oil Council and that because the acid levels were much lower than average for extravergine, by implication, this oil was "better than the best".

We visited some of the local groves and found that the trees were almost exclusively *Barnea* a variety that had been brought to New Zealand a decade earlier from Israel. We were puzzled at the lack of flavor from *Barnea* olives and when we returned to Italy we asked a professor from Perugia University whose expertise is the culture of olives. He said that he had found the same lack of flavor when assessing oil from the *Barnea*. He found that in Israel most of the olives are grown for eating. The locally produced oil tends to be made from the rejected table olives and these, combined with the warm ripening weather in autumn, results in a bland oil. It seems that there is little appreciation of strong flavors in olive oil. *Barnea* thrives in the desert climate and yields heavily and these attributes, not the criteria of flavor, make it popular.

Last year we were given another bottle of oil by a plant nutritionalist visiting from New Zealand. The producers had compensated for the lack of flavor by soaking lemons in the olive oil before bottling. It was a pleasant taste but faded rather quickly.

We remembered the bland oil we had used initially in Australia and how it had taken us quite a time (and eventually time in Italy) for us to develop an appreciation of just how important flavor is to olive oil. Many consumers in Anglo Saxon countries still lack this appreciation. But things are changing. For many years much of the oil imported to Australia and New Zealand has been bland, low grade oil, used mainly for cooking. In the past few years some Australians and New Zealanders have planted olive groves with flavor in mind and are beginning to produce better quality, fruitier oils. Food writers now try to describe the flavor as well as the utility of olive oil and this is influencing consumers to demand better quality oil.

Even in Northern Europe there has been until recently some reluctance on the part of retailers to show a concern for the flavor of the oil they sell. We have Austrian friends nearby who produce olive oil and who tried to sell their excellent oil in Innsbruk but found that consumers would not pay for quality. It was more profitable to sell their surplus to Italian blenders who use it to upgrade low flavored oils. A similar experience happened to other friends who took their Umbrian oil back to Oxford and found that the local shop could not see any reason why they should pay more for it than the cheap Spanish oil they were importing. Yet, other German neighbors have had their oil taken up by a retailer in Bavaria who gets a premium price for it because it has a fruity, spicy flavor.

It will not be long before the general consumer in Australia and New Zealand will acquire a taste for the bitter, spicy, and fruity oils that are the hallmarks of quality in Italy.

How are premium oils produced?

Central Italy produces some of the finest premium oils in the world. A quick examination of the specialty shops shows that these oils consistently fetch high prices. This claim will attract howls of protest from producers in other parts of Italy, and of course there are plenty of excellent oils produced in other places in the Mediterranean region but they will have to defend their own patch.

The Italians have conducted considerable research into the factors that make a premium oil and a great deal of this work has been done in Umbria at the University of Perugia and the experimental station at Spoleto. As local growers we have participated in courses provided by our local Comune and experts from these two institutions have come to help us understand and adopt best practice in olive grove management. Our small grove, made up of old abandoned and now recuperated trees and new trees we have planted ourselves shows a great improvement as a result.

Controllable factors for producing a premium oil

Variety plays a most important part in premium oil production. You will not get a premium oil from reject table olives or even the so-called dual purpose varieties. Even within the good oil producing varieties there is a considerable difference in the level of quality they contribute. In Central Italy we use four classic varieties for the production of premium oil, but each are of differing quality and growers balance the characteristics of yield, resistance to frost, and flavor to achieve the unique characteristics of Central Italian olive oil.

Once this balance of varieties is established there are a number of management factors that will affect oil quality.

Naturally low yielding olive trees on poor stony land produce better oil but deliberate action to reduce yield, as one does with vines to produce premium wine, is not used with olives.

Early picking is important. If the olives are left to late maturity many of the flavor components diminish. How far early picking can be used to overcome a natural lack of flavor caused by poor varieties or unsuitable climate is debatable. A fine judgment is needed here because picking too early will increase the bitter flavor caused by the polyphenols and improve the oil in the direction of more "bite" but can reduce the fruity flavors produced by esters and other chemicals. The overall balance of flavor is essential to good oil.

The fruit has to be harvested carefully, handled and stored with minimum damage, and then taken for processing within a day or two of picking because the flavor diminishes markedly the longer the fruit is stored.

The olives should be crushed without recourse to high temperatures or excessive amounts of water and after the oil is taken off the sediments it should be kept in containers in a cool, dark storeroom.

Uncontrollable factors

Temperature is an important contributor to flavor as well as yield, yet it is the largest uncontrollable factor that the grower must manage. This applies not just to the general climate for growing olives but the micro climate that produces premium oils. It is during autumn (in Italy this is September and October) that most of the oil is produced in the fruit. The flavor component of olive oil consists mainly of polyphenols, esters and aldehydes which are produced at the same time as the oil in the pulp of the olive fruit. Research shows that greater quantities of these flavor components are produced in zones that have a cool autumn.

If the day temperatures during this period rise no higher than 20 to 25°C conditions are perfect for the production of premium oils with lots of flavor. Olive oil contains a mixture of fats. The major one is oleic - derived from "olive". These temperature conditions are also ideal for the production of a high percentage of oleic (mono unsaturated) fat.

Of course quality is not guaranteed by good climatic conditions alone as the Marlborough experience with *Barnea* shows so clearly. Autumn weather conditions in this northern part of the South Island of New Zealand should be ideal for the production of a premium oil - they certainly are for premium white wine - but they obviously do not compensate for the effect of a variety that produces a bland oil.

A surprise to us was the tolerance and resistance olive trees have to cold winters. The winters in central Italy are very cold. We had often been here in winter as we needed to be in North Africa during the growing season for grain and pasture. We had shivered in the piazze of Florence where the fountains were frozen solid and on one Christmas Day the spray from the fountain at St Peter's in Rome was freezing on the pavement.

We have had snow on our farm every year during the decade we have lived here. In December 1996 it was nearly a metre deep. This was exceptional as we normally have only 5 to 10 cm perhaps two or three times during the winter and early spring. We are quite relieved when it snows as the temperature falls only a few degrees below zero and is not a hazard for the olives.

What we fear is the dry hard cold wind from Siberia - the dreaded Tramontana. This pushes the temperature much lower and causes frost damage to the olives. Most experts here say that -4°C is the end of the scale for frost resistance but we have found that the classic Tuscan and Umbrian varieties suffer little damage until the thermometer reaches -7° to - 8° C. Other varieties that originate in the mountains of central Umbria and Mt Amiata in Tuscany are more resistant still.

Temperature alone is not a measure of the damage. The length of time the trees are exposed to sub zero winds is also important. A snap overnight frost with the temperature down to -7° C for an hour or so is unlikely to cause any damage to the trees - at least in winter when they are dormant. When this temperature is maintained for two or three days damage is significant and trees can be lost. Tolerance during spring when there are fresh shoots on the trees is much lower. A temperature of -4° C , even overnight, will certainly scorch the young growth.

The older farmers around us remember all the great frosts. Really bad ones seem to occur every twenty five or thirty years. Then there is a total wipe out of the crop and many trees are totally frosted off above ground. Less severe frosts occur at about ten year intervals - we had one in 1996 which affected the leaves and younger wood of the more susceptible varieties. Our yield that year was about half our average.

It is the frequency of severe winter frost that acts as a limit to olive growing in central Italy and southern Europe generally. The higher one goes into the mountains the more frequently the trees are damaged or destroyed by frost. The economic cost in terms of yield is high.

As an example, we have a friend who is redeveloping an abandoned olive grove in the mountains above Assisi. At this altitude the olives are frosted more frequently and the previous owner found that they were uneconomic. Our friend crushes his own top quality oil and sells it through his winery for an excellent price of over $30 a litre. He is able to make the grove pay in spite of the frosts whereas the ordinary grower selling to a bottler for $15 a litre cannot.

On the plains in New Zealand the autumns are cool and should be ideal for premium olive oil production particularly in the north of the South Island. The winters do not become extreme until you move into the mountains of the Southern Alps. The lower slopes of these could provide areas suited to high quality oil production if the economics warrant it.

Even if an olive grove at this altitude proves not to be viable for a commercial grower, a hobby farmer with a direct sales outlet or some one with a few trees in the garden wanting to make oil for household use may find it worthwhile to take the climatic risk.

In Australia potential growers may find it more difficult to find optimum climatic conditions for the production of premium oil. The great central desert heats up much of the continent and growers will probably need to go into the hills or to the southern coasts or Tasmania to find autumns cool enough for top quality production. These areas do not usually suffer from severe winter frost damage because the winds from Antarctica are warmed (at least relatively!) by their long passage over the sea.

Soils

Soils or lack of them play an important part in the eventual result. Research into flavor has shown that oil produced on stony hillsides in Umbria has more than double the level of flavor components compared to those grown under the more lush growing conditions on the plains.

Rainfall

When olives are grown under conditions of natural rainfall, the amount of available water is uncontrollable. It is commonly believed that olives need to be stressed during the mid summer period. In the Mediterranean zone olives thrive on winter rainfall and summer drought. Olives are now being grown outside this climatic zone in China, northern NSW and Queensland where winters are dry and there is summer rainfall. Irrigation is being used by some growers either to establish olive groves or to encourage higher production. Some Italian experts have expressed concern about the impact of this on the eventual flavor of the oil but have admitted that it is as yet too early to say with certainty one way or the other.

Most of the olives in the Mediterranean are grown under rainfed conditions. Nearly all of Italy would be classed as "high rainfall" country by Australians. Most of Italy has an annual average rainfall of well above 500 mm. with the mountain areas receiving at least 1000 mm and some more than 2000 mm. There is small part of the south, of Sicily and of Sardegna which receives less than 500 mm. Here on our farm, we record an average of 800 mm which is about the mean for plain and hill country throughout Umbria and Tuscany. Premium oil comes from zones where rainfall averages are frequently higher than this and provided there is a dry stress period during the middle of summer, this high rainfall does not detract from quality. This is different from wine grapes where high rainfall or irrigation leads to excessive cropping and foliage and reduced quality unless controlled.

Olives grow in much lower rainfall zones on the southern shore of the Mediterranean and in Greece. In Tunisia they are grown without irrigation in areas with as little annual rainfall as 250 mm. In these very dry areas yield is low and erratic.

Irrigation of olives is becoming more common in Italy as growers try to increase production and bring trees to maturity earlier than in the past. We do not have any irrigation but a friend on the other side of our town irrigates his trees in spite of getting a higher rainfall than we do. His oil quality is excellent. He uses the irrigation to speed up the maturity of young trees. Young trees that are over-stressed have the irritating habit of dropping their fruit in late summer and this may continue for 5 or 6 years. He also uses the irrigation to improve fruit set in the spring and oil production in the autumn while still leaving a summer stress period.

So, what makes a premium oil?

After ten years experience here we can now say that premium oil is the result of a combination of a number of factors manipulated by individual growers. As we struggle each year with weather, with planting, pruning, fertilising, picking and pressing we find that every year there is a variation in the taste of our oil. Fundamentally it is good, but it will never, we hope, be uniform and predictable.

Chapter 3

LANDCARE AND TREECARE

Olives and mixed farming

On small farms in Umbria the olives are part of a mixed system. "Mixed" here is not the same as mixed farming in Australia or New Zealand. In the Barossa Valley we had a mixed farm with cereals, a vineyard, almonds, pistachios, Australian flowers and grazing. Except that the sheep grazed the cereal stubble each land use was quite separate. Here on our inherited olive grove the trees were planted 10 metres by 10 metres apart and two vines were planted in between each tree. Cereals were planted down the wide rows where the land was not too stony and other fruit trees, apples, cherries and walnuts, were interspersed here and there.

It is easy to dismiss this mixed system as a quaint piece of folk farming not suited to modern practices. For example, the frequent machine spraying of vines with copper would be wasteful as so much of the spray intended for the vines would go on the olive trees. Harvesting cereals down a 10 m row is obviously impractical with modern machinery and the herbicides used on cereals would damage the vines. In Italy today small farmers are advised to make new plantings of olives with higher tree density, say 6 metres x 6 metres.

Mixed systems should not be lightly dismissed altogether as a relic of folk farming. There is scientific justification for it. Scientists investigating the possibilities of agro-forestry have looked at some old farming systems from Africa and Asia. They have found that crops or pastures and trees actually utilise different parts of the environment and are complimentary rather than competitive. It sounds a little like perpetual motion but the trees tap into a different part of the soil profile than the pasture or crop. If this is applied to olives then there is some sense in the old system. Olives are pruned each year and thus do not cast deep shade over a companion crop or pasture. Two crops on the same land without reducing the output of either sounds too good to be true yet when olives are planted in 10 metre rows, sown pasture for grazing or hay is often a practical option.

Our neighbor, has a neat little agro-olive grove with well managed lucerne for hay production which he grows between the rows of olives. Other neighbors operate a more hit or miss system cutting the rough meadow between the trees, selling it in the spring to feedlotters or renting the uncut meadow for the grazing of horses.

Elsewhere there are big commercial olive groves on steep hillsides and they are not mixed with other crops.

Landcare in Umbria

Landcare is a brilliant word. So much more expressive than old fashioned "soil conservation". Sometimes we get the impression that land care does not rank high in the minds of modern Italian farmers. Much of the hill country throughout Italy - not just in Umbria - is badly eroded due to frequent cultivation to excessive depth.

The worst erosion is due to deep ploughing of cereals and other crops. Over the last fifty years in Italy, generous subsidies have kept the returns for cereals high and cheap money has been available to farmers to buy tractors and other farm machinery. Like all farmers in the world they have been unable to resist buying the biggest and most powerful machinery available and they use up enormous quantities of diesel driving these things around the tiny fields, ploughing the life out of the shallow top soil and dragging up stones and boulders from what appears to be the centre of the earth. To achieve a reasonable seed bed they have to make about five passages over the land - first of all creating havoc and then taming it. On any land that slopes slightly, let alone on hillsides, the result is horrendous erosion. Man-made erosion has caused more damage to agricultural land in Italy since the 1950s than the beginning of farming. An archaeologist friend, who is an expert on prehistoric European farming confirmed this on his dig near Gubbio in northern Umbria. He was able to measure the sediments that had collected on the site from the erosion of neighboring fields. Measurements from the last 1500 years indicated a layer of 20 to 30 cm and Roman farming before that created slightly more erosion but the post 1950 layer, which includes modern shards of broken Coca Cola bottles, is already 2 metres deep.

These are some lovely figures to toss around in a conversation but they only add precision to what we see after every heavy rain when torrents of rich muddy water pour down the ditches and any field that has been recently ploughed is scoured with rills. We always expect, or at least hope, that farmers will take some preventive action to avoid this but invariably the land is ploughed deep the next year.

Vineyards are also subject to serious erosion. Most of the vineyards are still being planted with the rows straight up and down the slope and they are also ploughed a number of times in the spring.

Cereals and vines seem to be worse culprits than olive groves. Most olive groves are left under grass and not ploughed but at a recent olive growers' meeting in our village one grower told us that his neighbor had been ploughing his olive grove to control weeds every spring for the last thirty odd years. It is on a moderate slope and was originally on the same level as his field of pasture. After thirty years of ploughing there is now a 15 cm step down his neighbor's olive grove.

In our olive grove it was landclear not landcare that was our first priority. When we bought the tractor and chopper we were delighted to find that we could do more in half an hour than we had done by hand in a couple of days. The tractor and trinciatore are a dramatic combination. We put the tractor into low gear, close our eyes, although this is not obligatory, and drive straight into the biggest blackberry bush and demolish it. Our blackberry bushes are often two metres high and four metres in diameter. The trinciatore (chopper) simply chews the bush up and spits out little chips a couple of centimetres long. Afterwards we spot spray the regrowth with Round-up in the spring. This clearing does not induce erosion and the material left behind adds organic matter and therefore nutrition to the soil. The natural legumes rapidly invade the cleared areas and they transform waste land into good pasture.

Cultivation or pasture?

Having cleared the debris we had to decide whether to cultivate each spring or not. The rough surface that the previous years of deep ploughing had caused was a real problem. It was almost impossible to mow efficiently, the field was hell to walk about on, and picking, which involved laying nets and carting boxes back and forth, was awkward and unnecessarily tiresome. We had one advantage when it came to making a decision, we weren't into deep ploughing and we had used shallow cultivation in Australia and we were able to buy in Italy a scarifier that would till the soil lightly. We were a bit worried about messing up the natural pasture that had grown undisturbed after the land was abandoned, and we were also worried about what cultivation would do to the wild orchids and other flowers and bulbs that flourished in the spring.

Once again, we talked to our neighbors. They told us that they plough

FACING PAGE: *An old olive grove, a new intensive grove and erosion gutters forming below it. Near Castello della Sala, Umbria.*

under the olive trees because it kills the weeds in spring and makes all the spring moisture available to the trees. If the ground remains bare then late spring rains provide moisture for the trees in early summer. Early ploughed soil also helps prevent damage from spring frosts as the bare soil absorbs the heat from the sun during the day and radiates it back at night.

We thought about it and then realised that there is another side to annual ploughing. Certainly ploughing under the trees to eliminate weeds can make more moisture available to the trees, but the cost is high. It eliminates the possibility of grazing or of cutting natural meadow or growing a crop for hay. On a single purpose olive grove planted at 6 x 6 metres the returns from grazing may not be significant compared to the production of olive oil but for a more widely spaced grove the loss can be important.

Overriding these considerations of profit is the undoubted risk of erosion. A couple of light cultivations in a single year will do little damage to the soil structure but ploughing every year is certainly going to lead to serious erosion. Ploughing the natural pasture in spring prevents plants from seeding. Once the seed reserves have been depleted year after year the natural pasture will disappear. Even persistent weeds will give up and the ground will be left unprotected in autumn and winter and vulnerable to water erosion. With no organic matter being returned to the soil, its structure will deteriorate, runoff will have an easier path to take, and erosion will rapidly wash the soil away.

We have seen the terrible destructive effect of constant ploughing in olive groves in southern Spain. In some badly eroded groves trees grow on little mounds where the roots of the olive hold some soil while the rest has been washed away. It is interesting that the first use of Australian medic and sub clover pastures in Spain and Portugal was to try to restore the thrashed soils under olive trees. In Tunisia there is also terrible wind erosion in the areas with sandy soils and low rainfall.

The benefits to the trees of moisture conservation credited to ploughing are somewhat unpredictable. Ironically, the best moisture storage is achieved in the zone where it is least needed. In the higher rainfall zone, such as Umbria and most of central Italy, there is a completely wet soil profile by the end of winter but because the spring rains are reasonably secure it is a rare season indeed when extra moisture is needed. In the really dry zone winter rainfall is sparse and uncertain and it is rare that moisture storage is significant. Certainly it is not enough to justify exposing these fragile soils to the erosion caused by removing the natural plant cover.

Watching the deep erosion in our garden, on our hillside and in our fields that became worse after every heavy downpour we had in our first years here, we decided that erosion control had to be uppermost in our minds.

But we first had to level out the furrows left by years of deep ploughing if we were to achieve ease of movement in our olive grove. This meant a program of shallow cross cultivation for a year or more. This has led to quite an improvement. The surface of the land is more even and we and our various implements move more easily around it. We have now left the grove to revert to grass and legumes which we will mow in spring and summer. The bulbs and other wildflowers are reappearing.

We have not gone deeper than 8 to 10 cm. when cross cultivating, but the usual depth used by farmers here is 25 cm. At a recent growers' meeting the visiting expert from Perugia advised shallow cultivation to a depth of no more than 8 cm. but as farmers use ploughs and not scarifiers cultivating to a depth of 8 cm is going to be difficult for them.

Pasture under the trees

Once the ground was level we began to encourage pasture under our trees. Because we do not want to create more competition with the olives than is necessary we have not sown lucerne or deep rooted perennial grasses but have encouraged a pasture of annual legumes such as local sub clover, wild vetch, medic and a range of wild flowers and native grasses. These annual legumes provide adequate nitrogen for the trees. As a means of encouraging what already grows there we mow the tall grass and apply some phosphate. After a couple of years we now have a flourishing pasture of natural medics and clovers. The native legumes certainly flourish when provided with the right encouragement.

It is rather a sad reflection on the slow pace of transmission of agricultural knowledge that Italian olive books we have read mention sub clover as a possible green manure for olives but have not yet caught up with medics which will be more useful under olives given that they and olives prefer alkaline soils. Amos Howard brought sub clovers into mainstream agriculture through his work in South Australia more than a century ago and now these Mediterranean clovers hover on the edge of European agricultural knowledge, but medics which have been in the scientific literature for a mere sixty or seventy years have yet to penetrate the established wisdom and remain very much on the specialist fringe.

Grazing in olive groves

Pasture flourishes best when it is grazed in winter. Grazing keeps the grass down and encourages the clover or medic. Grazing increases the amount of organic matter returned to the soil.

It is difficult to find sheep or cattle to graze pasture in our zone. These days few livestock in Italy graze in the open. There has been a leap from the old system of grazing with shepherds to intensive livestock production where animals live in sheds day and night and are fed grain and hay. In the old days on the little hill farms of central Italy, cattle were used to draw the cart and plough, sheep grazed under the olives and ate the cereal stubble, while pigs were grazed in the forest where they survived on roots and acorns.

When the share farming system collapsed in the 1950's, the young people (some of whom would have become shepherds) went to Switzerland to work as builders' labourers and the landowners, deprived of ample cheap labour, simply abandoned the land to blackberries.

When the largesse of the Common Agricultural Policy made farming pay again it did nothing to encourage grazing. Most farmers found that growing specific crops and later "set-aside" (under which grazing is forbidden) was the best proposition and so grazing with few exceptions faded from sight. To an Australian eye it is incredible to see many thousand and thousands of hectares of natural grazing being wasted and just being left each year as a bushfire hazard.

We do not have any animals so we have to mow our pasture in spring and summer. We leave most of the cut pasture as a mulch on the soil and gather some of it to heavily mulch young trees and save a bit for the garden compost bin.

If sheep are available to graze the pasture there may be a problem of tree damage. When sheep grazed under olives in this zone years ago they had shepherds to control them. On our farm in Australia the sheep certainly trimmed up the lower limbs of the olive trees but it was hardly a fair trial as the trees were near the house and shearing shed and there would often be many hundreds of hungry sheep in a small paddock for a few days as they waited to be shorn or treated. In North Africa and the Near East they say vehemently that sheep do eat olive trees, but as we know well from our own work there, the bare fallow used in that region leaves the flocks with hardly a blade of grass for months and in desperation they will attack anything that looks edible.

We believe that if sheep are grazed at a moderate stocking rate in the olive grove while the pasture is green they will not eat the trees. Our Italian olive books say that it is safe to let sheep, hens and turkeys graze under olives.

We have horses in our district and they are put out to graze in local groves. Although they sometimes damage young trees by rubbing they seem to leave the mature trees alone. Grazing is a good management technique if it can be arranged as it encourages a high legume content in the pasture and the return of nitrogen and other nutrients to the soil. Does it matter if the lower limbs of the trees are trimmed? If they are your sheep or horses, you may feel the occasional nibble is a low price to pay for the benefit of the grazing, but in a commercial grove it may be better not to risk it.

Passing sheep or cattle may be a hazard if trees are planted along roadsides or water ways and it may be necessary to use tree guards until they are tall enough to escape damage. Rabbits may be a problem in some areas of Australia. We are lucky that we have no rabbits to ring bark our young trees. We do have plenty of wild pigs and porcupines that come down from the surrounding forest but they do not attack olive trees although they churn up the ground in the olive grove in winter looking for the roots of docks and bulbs.

Cutting hay

Our olive grove is only just getting to the stage where we can cut and rake hay and plenty of our neighbors do this as a regular way of keeping the grass down. As our average rainfall is over 800 mm there is little risk of destroying our annual legumes when we cut our hay each spring. If we were in a drier zone we would have to consider topping the pasture to avoid taking off too much seed.

Nitrogen fertiliser

Olives in the Mediterranean zone are usually grown without any fertiliser, but there is no doubt that olives respond to fertilisers. At first we used the recommendations of our books on olives and applied a special NPK fertiliser for olives with 12% nitrogen. NPK for cereals contains 18% nitrogen. Application rates were difficult to work out in our widely spaced grove but we decided to use the 3 to 4 kg per tree as recommended. We worked out that if this formula was applied to a grove with a 6 X 6 m. planting we would have to apply 750 to 1000 kg per ha which seemed to us (based on Australian experience) to be grossly excessive. We had to admit that the trees responded well to the 3 to 4 kg of NPK. They looked a healthy dark green color and the smaller trees in particular had a much heavier crop.

We worked out a different regime for our new trees. We plant our new trees at two years of age and apply a bit less than 0.5 kg. of NPK per tree. Then we increase this to 1 kg. until they are five years old. Olives are slow to come into bearing and the NPK fertiliser pushes them along. More of the nitrogen goes into foliar growth than into the crop but this is not a bad thing at this stage. After five years growth we stop using the NPK and revert to the regime that we have found suits the mature trees. Our encouragement of native legumes provides us with sufficient nitrogen to keep the trees healthy and productive.

Phosphate fertiliser

To encourage the legumes we apply 100 kg of triple super per ha. over the whole area in autumn. In the spring we apply another 100 to 150 kg per ha. of triple super close to the trees. We use this formula because our trees were planted on a wide 10 X 10 m. grid.

Trace elements

Leaf analysis is is an excellent way of refining fertiliser application rates and sorting out the minor elements but that so far we haven't seen any signs of marked deficiencies in our trees so we have not undertaken it.

Some groves suffer from potash deficiency but our soils are not deficient in potash so we have no need to add more.

Our Italian olive book also says that magnesium and boron are important minor elements for olives and the NPK mix we buy for our olives has these elements added. We don't seem to have any deficiency in these trace elements either but if we do start seeing signs we will go back to the NPK + B + Mg olive mix once every few years just to be on the safe side. Alternatively we may be able to buy the minor elements and mix them ourselves.

In Spain they have had excellent results from the application of boron specially on calcareous soils. Boron in these soils remains locked in due to the high pH and not much is freed up to be available to the trees. Under these boron deficient conditions a foliar application of 20 to 30 gm. of boron in a soluble form is said to increase yields by two or three times. The symptoms of acute boron deficiency are leaves discolored at the tips, leaves shed prematurely, branches suffering die-back, and low yield. Fruit is deformed or corky and much falls to the ground. We do not have any of these symptoms so we reckon we are safe.

Most of the books written in English mention that olives are particularly tolerant to boron. Of course this is true but it misses the point which is that they are susceptible to boron deficiency. It shows how translations can subtly change the meaning.

Organic matter

Another fertiliser that is commonly used in Italy on olives is the NPK mixture (plus Mg and B.) with some added organic matter in the form of peat. We cannot see the point of this fertiliser as the amount of organic matter is so small that even if you applied 600 to 800 kg/ha of fertiliser it would have virtually no impact on the structure of the soil. A pasture under the trees should add 5,000 kg/ha or more organic matter to the soil each year and will improve the soil structure quite rapidly.

When there was more mixed farming the olives received a share of the animal manure as the animals went into stables at night and during bad weather in the winter. The stockpiled manure was dug in around the olive trees every year. Not many farmers these days keep sheep for milk and cheese, nor a pig for Christmas cheer and winter stores, but some farmers still use animal manure. They buy it in or get it from a cousin or a nearby livestock owner. It can also be bought at the garden centres, sterilised and matured - just the thing for the garden pots, but a little too expensive for the olive grove.

Pest and diseases

In spite of being grape growers in the Barossa we took one look at the spraying program for grapes in central Italy and said there must be an easier crop to grow and we took on olives. The local grape growers coat their vines with copper and sulphur frequently throughout the spring and summer until the leaves take on a blue hue. The amount of fungicide is certainly excessive but at least three or four applications are needed in most seasons. Olives certainly suffer from pests and diseases but unlike vines, which become more and more prone to attack by fungus diseases in cooler and damper climates, olives have fewer problems. This is confirmed by the survival of the olive and the fig on abandoned farms. Vines tend to die because they become riddled with chronic fungus disease once the spraying stops but olive trees linger on and on and on.

We have seen a few olive trees sprayed with copper fungicide in winter near Orvieto but it is not common and the great majority of olive trees in this zone are not sprayed at all. This could be developed into a marketing advantage as freedom from fungicides and insecticides allows growers to attach a "biologically produced" sticker to their label.

The pest that the local farmers speak of with dread is the olive fly which is *Dacus oleae*. This infects the fruit in zones with warmer autumns than ours and reduces the quality of the oil severely. It is controlled by the use of traps containing lures or, if the infection is already established, by the use of insecticides.

New Zealand growers have already experienced the disaster that strikes if imported stock is not rigorously screened for disease. In 1998 it was discovered that olive knot (either *Pseudonomas savastanoi* pv *savastanoi* or *Pseudonomas savastanoi* pv *neri*) was carried in on a batch of imported stock and distributed before it was detected. The imports had been quarantined for six months before being released in New Zealand but identification had not been made of the disease. Both types of olive knot cause reduced yield and falling leaves and results in tumours or knots on the twigs and branches that eventually kills the trees. The bacteria is insidious and survives in the knots from where rainfall picks up exuded matter and spreads it about. Wind can carry the disease a short distance when it is contained in raindrops. Cutting the knots off and applying therapeutic treatment can control the disease. In New Zealand a variation of the disease known as *Pseudonomas syringea* pv *savastanoi* has been detected on oleander bushes.

Generally though olives are rarely subject to the multiplicity of diseases and insects that ravage vine crops and for this we are duly thankful.

Chapter 4

PLANTING A NEW OLIVE GROVE

Living on the edge

The excellent quality of our oil is due to our cool autumns but these are followed by even colder winters and destructive frosts that can be fatal to young trees. When we planted our new trees we found just how close we are in our valley to the edge of climatic tolerance for olive trees .

Even before we had fully cleared the old trees of their accumulated jungle, we planted about half a dozen new trees on the edge of the grove and they seemed to grow well.

In 1996 when our the clearing program was complete we did our first big planting of 50 trees. By the autumn of that year we were very pleased with ourselves. We had not lost a single tree from either of these plantings. Judicious hand watering in the summer avoided losses due to drought.

Just after Christmas that year the frost struck. We had nearly a metre of snow and before that temperatures were below zero for four days. For long periods it hovered around -8°C. The cold was so severe that it killed wood up to two or three years old. The mature trees lost their leaves and their new fruiting wood but these trees recovered over the next two years. The older wood, protected by thicker layers of bark, did not suffer.

The new trees had no older bark protecting the wood and, to our horror, about a third of these were killed completely. Another third suffered badly and are still limping along. Some of these were killed above ground but they have shot again from the root and are nearly back to the size they were when planted two years ago. Others have regrown so slowly that we have replaced them with new stock. The slow regrowth was due to the fact they were effectively half or two-thirds ring barked by the frost. Now they are older some of this frosted bark is beginning to peel away and we can clearly see the extent of the frost damage.

This did not deter us from further planting but it did cause us to think carefully about the cold resistance of the varieties we chose for the next big expansion.

The layout of the grove

The previous owner had planted our grove in the traditional manner. The olive trees were spaced 10 m by 10 m, two vines were planted between the olives in the rows, and cereals were grown down the rows.

Each vine had a solid oak post alongside on which to grow. Near the top, angled holes were drilled and pegs half a metre long driven into them. The vine was then trained up the post and out on the pegs. We have been told that this is an imitation of an even older method pioneered by the Etruscans thousands of years ago when they trained their vines up small trees. The post with its angled pegs is intended to imitate a tree and branches. By the time we came along most of the vines in our grove were dead.

We pulled out what was left and thought about running a few dozen sheep to utilise the pasture we encouraged under the olive trees but this seemed to be a lot of effort for little return. Fences and a sheep yard would be needed - a considerable investment for a small number of animals. Not many sheep remain in our area and the two neighbors who have them milk them and make pecorino (sheep's) cheese. The thought of getting up at dawn on frosty mornings to milk ewes did not appeal.

Since we had to manage the whole grove in any case, it seemed sensible to increase the density of our plantings of olive trees. On our poor soil we did not think that it would be feasible to intensify the planting too much. We could see that competition from the old trees would make it difficult for the young trees to flourish. We therefore planted a new low density row between each of our existing rows. We now have rows 5 m apart and trees every 10 m in the rows or 50 sq m per tree.

The modern planting density in this zone for new single purpose olive groves is 6 m by 6 m. or 36 sq m per tree. There have been experiments with higher density plantings. It is claimed that the high density planting produces a faster return on investment. More is spent on trees but the return on the funds invested in the land is quicker. In Europe land is expensive and the idea, in theory, has considerable merit. In our part of Umbria few olive growers have mortgages and the economic argument does not seem to convince them. They see an olive grove as a long term investment - something that will see them out and will still be going strong for their children. They also know that it is easier to work a grove where the trees are reasonably well spaced.

The effect of terrain on the new grove

Paintings, frescoes and photographs of Umbria taken over the years show us that the old olive groves were planted on the poorer stony soil.

The best land was reserved for higher value crops particularly wheat. Our farm of 7 ha. had to support three share farming families consisting of 15 to 20 people who had to feed themselves and give half their produce to the landlord. It was sensible to grow food crops on the better land and put olives where nothing much else would thrive.

This has been a sensible and environmentally sound tradition. It has given us the premium oil for which Umbria is famous.

In Umbria and Tuscany many of the famous producers make great play of the fact that their groves are planted on extremely stony hillsides. The figures for Tuscany show that 7% of the groves are on the better soils of the plains, 83% on more or less steep hillsides and 10% in the mountains. We have a couple of good trees that appear to be growing out of a heap of loose stones dumped over the side of our track. While the poor stony land does produce the top quality oil, and this is a good selling point if the oil is sold direct from the grove gate, one must also remember that the yields are low. The difficulty facing local growers is that they do not always get a sufficiently large premium price from the oil buyers for that extra bit of quality obtained from really poor stony soil.

Today, however, there is a large surplus of cereal land in Umbria and throughout Europe encouraged by the policy of "set-aside". The policy makers have decided it is cheaper to quarantine land out of production for a fixed fee rather than pay the subsidies on the potential output. Canny farmers have succeeded in outmanoeuvring the bureaucrats by taking out of production their worst - almost abandoned - land but the bureaucrats are fighting back with tougher rules to make it more difficult to claim permanent "set aside" fees for cereal fields.

Some growers are now planting olives on well drained cereal land. Certainly the olives will grow faster and yield more on these deeper more fertile soils but the quality of the oil may not be quite as good.

We cursed our stony, alkaline, clay soil when developing our garden, but it has proved capable of producing very good oil. Heavy clay on its own is not so good and south of Siena, where clay is very heavy, olives do not thrive. Acid soils of less than pH 5 are equally inhospitable to olives. Apart from this, olives seem to have a pretty good tolerance of soil types. We have seen olives grown in pure sand in Tunisia and Libya. In fact North African growers are told that olives are particularly well suited to these light textured soils although (in a throw away line) "they will also grow in clay".

Waterlogging

Everyone is agreed that olives cannot stand waterlogging but this doesn't mean that they aren't happy with a high rainfall. Our average rainfall is 800 mm which is not a great deal in central Italy. Many of the famous olive growing areas in the mountains have double this amount and more. The rain falls mainly in the autumn and spring. In midwinter we usually have a dry period in January and February. Summers are dry. We frequently have periods of perhaps a week when we receive as much as 75 mm of rainfall and the olive grove is oozing with water. Our grove is on a slope and drains well. It is of course absolutely saturated at times but the water is on the move and the olives do not suffer.

Where drainage is poor or doesn't exist, then waterlogging prevents olives growing. This is one of the reasons they are not grown in the bottom of the valleys in Umbria.

Irrigation

We have a well that provides us with 1500 litres of clean water a day or, as we put on the underground water survey questionnaire, "one teaspoon per second". It is plenty for the house, just enough for the garden pots and a few privileged flowers and vegetables, and totally inadequate for any sustained irrigation of the olives or other fruit trees. Irrigation, therefore, was not an option for us so we had to follow the norm in the Mediterranean basin and leave our trees to the vicissitudes of natural rainfall.

We do however water our young olive trees with 15 litres of water carted to each tree a couple of times in summer for the first and sometimes the second year. Obviously a drip irrigation system would give us better early growth.

In areas with low rainfall, irrigation will improve yields and the reliability of yields. If it is used skilfully there should not be a reduction in the quality of the oil.

The objective is to overcome any spring or winter drought, not to lessen normal summer stress.

Choosing the varieties

The choice of variety, as with most crops, is a balancing act between quality and yield - that is yield of oil, not the fresh yield of olives. Without quality varieties it will be impossible to produce quality oil.

We are hobby olive growers. We do not depend on selling oil. We are more interested in the quality than quantity of the oil but we still want to get some reasonable return for our efforts. We therefore favored varieties that would produce high quality oil. We had also to make sure that they were as frost resistant as possible.

Varietal names

There are hundreds of varieties grown in central Italy. To the foreigner the picture appears to be total confusion but many of these "varieties" are merely different local names for the same tree. A couple of years ago we planted some *Dolce agogia*, a very common variety from Perugia which is only one line of hills over from us. We employed our usual team of "moonlighting" road workers to help us plant. They were totally baffled by this *"Dolce agogia"* and wondered if it was something we had imported from Australia but when talking to other growers we found it is widely planted here but under a different local name.

The picture is becoming more complex because new varieties of varieties are coming onto the market to take advantage of plant variety rights. One of the recent ones in *Minerva* which is a selection from *Leccino* and is claimed to be more frost resistant.

Making the choice

Aside from local names and "new" varieties there are still many hundreds of varieties available. Among these are four major classic varieties grown for quality oil in central Italy. They are *Frantoio* (it means the oil mill), *Leccino*, *Moraiolo*, and *Maurino*. *Frantoio* and *Moraiolo* have more flavor than the other two. Growers plant different mixes of these varieties in different parts of central Italy - in Umbria we grow more *Moraiolo,* while they grow more *Frantoio* in Tuscany.

Of course in naming these we are putting our heads on the chopping block as there will be many experts prepared to argue for the inclusion of this or that variety as one of the "classics". Those we named could be considered as the olive oil equivalent of *Shiraz*, *Cabernet Sauvignon* and *Grenache* to the South Australian red wine industry.

Years ago when growing grapes in the Barossa Valley we had to make a trade-off between quality and quantity when we chose the grape varieties for our vineyard. We could plant relatively low yielding but high quality *Cabernet Sauvignon* or we could choose the higher yielding but lesser quality *Shiraz*. At the bottom of the scale of quality was *Grenache* which yielded double the quantity of *Shiraz*. Most growers would juggle with these according to the prices or the demand of the wineries for quality grapes.

Olive growers around us have always planted a mixture of varieties in their groves. *Frantoio* and *Moraiolo* produce higher quality oil than *Leccino* but the yields are about the same. *Leccino* (to which *Dolce agogia* is similar) is popular because it is more frost resistant than the other two and is a tough variety that resists many pests and diseases. *Pendolino* is a local variety that is highly prized as a good pollinator and is usually included. Older olive groves usually contain a few local unnamed ecotypes and growers value these because they claim they add to the flavor of the oil.

Growers in Australia and New Zealand will face a more difficult choice if the widely used Israeli variety *Barnea* lives up to the claims of its promoters and produces yields of 20 tonnes/ha of fresh fruit. Even if the oil percentage is not high the yield of oil will be enormous, if of indifferent quality, and growers will be facing a choice similar to the wine grape grower's of *Sultana* versus *Sauvignon Blanc* decision.

Aiming for oil yield and taste is the first criteria but other factors will influence the choice of variety such as pollination, potential yield and fruit size.

Pollination

Our realisation of the importance of pollination came when we were in New Zealand staying with our daughter who had, on the advice of her local nursery, planted a row of the Israeli variety *Barnea* near the road that passed by her vineyard. When we saw them the trees were five years old but had failed to produce a single fruit. The trees were lush and robust but had not been seriously pruned. At first we thought it was the lack of light; but there were signs that they had flowered well but no mature fruit had resulted. We were pretty sure that the explanation was lack of pollination.

When we planted our first few new trees in our own grove, our nursery had mentioned pollination but as we were planting into an old mixed variety grove it seemed not important.

When we got back home we discovered that most Italian varieties - and obviously *Barnea* from our daughter's experience - set a low volume of fruit until pollinated by another variety and even where they are self pollinating to some degree it is not considered worth the risk of planting them alone because of the potential failure to pollinate in poor seasons.

Maurino has been shown to be a particularly good pollinator as it has a long period of pollen production.

Research in Italy has shown that when groves are planted to only one of the four classic Umbrian/Tuscan varieties self pollination produces less than 1% of fertilised flowers. If a single pollinator is planted in the grove the rate increases to about 3% which is quite adequate to produce a good crop in an average year. With more varieties in the grove the rate of fertilised flowers is on average 5% which provides a safety margin in those years when the weather conditions are too hot or too cold, or the wind too strong, or there is fog or rain at the wrong time.

This research has led to changes in the recommendations for planting and it is now considered prudent to plant a pollinator within a 20 to 30 metre range of each tree.

Scientific research has confirmed the wisdom of the "old timer's" method of planting groves with a mixture of varieties.

Varieties and Oil yield

The excellent **"Olive Production Manual"** from the University of California gets itself into a real muddle when it tries to rank varieties in terms of specific oil percentages. Choosing a variety because it has been designated with a measurement of oil percentage higher than another variety can be misleading.

Calculation of the yield of oil from each variety reflects the oil percentage and the yield of fresh fruit and these vary depending on seasonal conditions, soil type, and when the fruit is picked. Early picking will result in a lower percentage of oil and later picking will result in a higher percentage of oil but from less weight of fruit. The yield from both picks will be practically the same. Very late picking will produce even higher oil percentages, but because the fruit starts to fall on the ground if left too late, the yield of oil for the grove will actually decline.

In our grove within any two years the variation of oil percentage can be between 14 and 18% from the same trees. In some years one variety will yield more oil than the other and vice versa in the following year.

Italian experts do not follow the Californians in codifying oil percentages from individual varieties with specific numbers, instead they rank them as high, moderate and low.

The method of processing can affect the yield of oil from whatever variety or mix of varieties. We will describe processing in more detail later in the book but at this stage suffice to say that pushing up the temperature at the frantoio will extract as much as 2% more oil from the fruit but at a price of reduced quality. We have been told by the oil quality experts to expect on average no more than 15% oil in our zone. If we get higher percentages - certainly if it edges up to 20% - we should be wary as the frantoio is probably increasing the temperature and using other tricks to extract more oil but at the cost of reducing the quality.

Fruit size and mechanised picking

Selecting varieties for fruit size can be important if you intend to use a mechanical shaker when harvesting. The shaking method of olive harvesting has limited value for the production of quality oil because efficient harvesting can only take place during the late harvest period when the flavor components of the olive are in decline. However future improvements may make the machines able to cope with relatively immature fruit and it may be worth keeping this in mind when choosing varieties as olives are slow growing and replanting to gain fruit size will take a long time.

Fruit of less than 1.5 to 2.0 gm in weight will not be harvested efficiently by shakers at any time. Fortunately our local classic varieties all pass this test, but there are a couple of varieties that are even better for mechanical picking according to advisers from the University of Perugia. *Carolea* and *Coratina* that are grown in the south of Italy combine good oil quality with large fruits in the 4 to 5 gm range. Local growers seem to be content to plant our existing varieties to judge from the stock currently available at our local nurseries.

Varieties and taste

The names of the varieties from which the oil comes do not appear on the bottle because, at present, oil is labelled on a district basis. The controls on district labelling do state that there must be minimum amounts of the specified named varieties in the oil and that they must be grown within the district boundaries.

Some producers are beginning to mention the varieties on their labels. If they follow the trend set in the wine industry, varietal labelling will become more common.

Of course these four classic varieties are not the only quality varieties in the world. Other countries and other parts parts of Italy have their own quality varieties. In central Italy we tend to be a little snooty about oils from

FACING PAGE: A young tree showing four upward growing laterals that will form the frame of the wine glass. The main trunk has been stopped.

other regions and refer to them as "dolce" or sweet in a tone of contempt. They are not really "sweet" - in fact soft would be a better description - but they lack the bitter and peppery tastes of Umbrian and Tuscan oils. While they may not appeal to us they are well thought of elsewhere and could well prove popular in countries such as Australia and New Zealand which currently import large quantities of bland, almost tasteless oils. It may take time for the consumer to appreciate the stronger flavors of our hill grown olives.

Assessing the nursery stock

Strangers can see things that are hidden to those that live with them all their lives. When we bought our trees we went to the local nursery and bought two-year-old olive trees and planted them as they were. This is what everyone else does here.

The trees had a single trunk. At a height of 1.2 metres the lateral branches were trained to form the bowl of the "wine glass". Below this was some straggly fruiting wood hanging down. The Italian trees have been trained to a single stem by ruthless rubbing off of shoots and all the growth has been pushed into this single leader. The single stem is not strong so it needs to be well supported by a stake.

It all appeared so simple and straightforward but when we got to New Zealand we realised that it represented considerable skill in the nursery. Many of the trees we saw had been allowed to grow untended in the nurseries and the result was little furry bushes more like a box hedge than an olive tree. Half a dozen leaders competed with each other and in spite of vigorous growth were often no more than 50 cm. high after a couple of years. The energy of the tree had gone outwards instead of upwards.

Planting

Having chosen the most suitable varieties and obtained the best young trees available, we then got to dig holes. Dig a hole, dig it anywhere on our farm, to any depth and you will find someone has been there before you. We always hope for treasure, a copper coin, or at least a piece of glazed pottery, but the farmers in the hills of Umbria have always been too poor for such luxuries and we find broken bricks and tiles and, occasionally, pieces of unglazed pot. The previous owner of our grove found two beautifully worked Neolithic arrow heads when he was ploughing, but we've had no luck so far.

The local advice and the Italian olive books all say that you should deep rip or dig holes to 80 cm. or a metre. We can understand if there is a specific impermeable layer of clay or rock that needs to be broken up, but to do it as a matter of course implies that the olive tree has a weak root system that needs assistance to penetrate the ground. All the circumstantial evidence points in the other direction. Olives seem to grow in the toughest environments.

We suspect that deep ripping or deep digging is linked to the European obsession with deep ploughing rather than any scientifically proven need. Ancient Greek writers recommended deep holes in which to plant olive trees and, while it is tempting to say that two and a half thousand years of experience can't be wrong, the same writers said that ewe lambs were conceived when the wind came from the south and rams when it blew from the north. Perhaps they are right about that too?

We compromised on planting depth. We contracted a neighbor to come in and dig holes of 30 to 40 cm deep with his backhoe. In the aftermath we recovered some wonderful stones for our garden. We've also found that some pockets in the strata do not drain well and we made sure to avoid these when planting our new trees.

We plant our trees in the holes with a mixture of sand and potting mix to lighten up the cloddy clay that is difficult to consolidate around the roots of young trees.

We keep a close eye on them for the first few months so that we can give them water before they become stressed. Our summers tend to creep up on us and a few hot days can stress young trees quite badly.

Pruning the young trees

When our new trees were frosted off at ground level after the 1996 frost bush growth re-emerged but we intervened rapidly in the spring and again two or three times during the following summer to rub off the surplus shoots and leave a single leader without competition.

To keep the shape we found that we had to pay particular attention to the normal early pruning as well. We looked for three or four laterals with which to form a nicely shaped wine glass and just above these the pruning cut to the main trunk was made. Of course trees vary and sometime you find only two strong laterals. This is not a disaster as further branching of the laterals will fill in the wine glass.

With young trees we take more care to eliminate overlapping branches than we would in mature trees. It is quite a challenge to keep the centre clear and keep checking the laterals so that they grow up in a series of zig zags rather than a single upward dash as they would prefer.

This constant stopping of the upward growing shoots will encourage the growth of the "straggly bits" which form the skirt where most of the fruit will be.

The first fruit

Fruit should appear in the first year or so, but of course, it will only be a small handful to begin with. After five years the first decent crop should appear, but this will depend very much on the fertility of the soil and the seasons in between. In our case, we have had quite nice handfuls of fruit from some of our young trees but the severe frost has delayed the maturity of the trees and we will have to wait for another couple of years before we can really start to count on a higher yield due to more trees in our olive grove. One of the first words we learned in Italy was "Pazienza" - (patience), and, with olives, there is no doubt that a lot of it is needed.

Chapter 5

RECUPERATING OLD TREES AND PRUNING

Clearing the jungle

In our first year here we set off with baskets and ladders to pick our olives with great enthusiasm, until we put our heads into the jungle that entangled the trees. The olives were so sparse, the picking took so long, and the amount of oil was so miserable, that we nearly abandoned the whole olive grove to the blackberries and old man's beard that dominated it. Thrusting through this undergrowth, avoiding prickles and being torn by thorns was not the best way to enjoy an olive harvest. The olives kept getting lost in the thickets and it was impossible to spread nets under the trees as everyone else was doing. So what to do? There appeared to be good crops on nearby trees and our neighbors seemed to think that olive growing was worth the effort. This gave us new heart and we set out to discover how to go about improving our olive grove. It was obvious that we needed not only to clear the undergrowth but also to get a more practical shape into our abandoned trees. They were misshapen, full of dead wood and extremely difficult to pick.

Shaping the trees

Our trees were more or less abandoned soon after 1985 when there had been a disastrous frost throughout central Italy. In our part of Umbria the temperature had fallen to between -10°C and - 15°C for days on end. Other parts of Umbria and Tuscany recorded even lower temperatures. Many of our olive trees were completely killed above ground but the frames of others survived although smaller wood was destroyed and no leaves remained. The previous owner of our grove had cut off the dead trunks and limbs with a chainsaw but after that he seems to have lost heart and left the trees to their own devices. Some trees had regrown from their roots into multi-stem bushes. The trees that survived above ground had just gone on growing up and up. The small crop they had could only be reached with long ladders. The bottom half of the trees were a mass of dead twigs.

There were olive trees on our farm in the Barossa Valley planted around the homestead by my great grandfather many years ago and they had shown the same characteristics. Trees that had been cut down, perhaps after they had been burnt in some bush fire, left roots that remained vigorous and thick bushes of a hundred stems grew from them. Other trees must have been pruned years ago into a wine glass shape but had been neglected for decades and these had become very tall and quite unwieldy. Yields were low and the fruit was small.

Looking at our Umbrian neighbors' groves here we saw that they had reshaped the bushy regrowth on their trees by cutting off most of the stems and leaving only three or four to become new trunks. They built a new bowl shape from these.

With a new tree, the bowl is formed above a single stem or trunk which is trained to grow about a metre high before branching out. This is the wine glass shape that is the standard practice in Italy. With badly frosted trees, if the old single trunk is killed, it is cut off with the chainsaw and a new bowl is formed straight from the ground without the stem. It is possible to leave only a single trunk and reshape the bowl above but this delays a return to full bearing. There is also a risk that the tree will fall over in a strong wind because the suckers that form the trunks of the multi-stem tree are not always well attached to the old stump and can break off. If three or four stems are left and one is lost, it is not a complete disaster. The group of stems also shelter each other from the effects of strong winds.

The decision about which three or four stems to use is not easy. It caused us great anguish as the regrowth often consists of fifteen to twenty stems and to a novice this is a daunting cut to make. We were fearful that we would either cut out the best stems or leave the tree so demoralised that it would die in despair. Fortunately, we found out that olive trees love stress and enjoyed the big cut enormously.

Time of pruning

In Italy, we prune in late winter - February and March . It is the period of maximum dormancy for olives. Some growers with large estates start earlier - in fact not long after picking finishes in December - and they are often still pruning into the beginning of April. If pruning goes on later than this the sap is rising and the cuts bleed excessively.

When we had the heavy frost damage on our farm in December 1996 we did not prune until May 1997 because it was extremely difficult to tell which wood was completely dead and which had only lost its leaves. We wanted to be sure that we were not cutting off potentially good fruiting wood unnecessarily and we could only be sure by waiting until the trees shot in late spring.

Frost damage usually causes trees to push out large numbers of water shoots (or suckers) from dormant buds in the main branches and from the base of the trunk. Some of these can be used to reshape the tree but most will have to be cut off. Most growers do this during the summer because to leave them to grow on wastes energy that can be better used to strengthen the retained shoots and assist the yield of new fruit.

Growers who use irrigation tell us that they have an enormous amount of vegetative growth on their trees during spring and summer. They routinely carry out a second pruning in August to thin the trees and improve the initiation of flower buds which takes place in September. We, of course, don't have this problem as our olives grow on shallow soil over stones and our summer period is dry.

Years ago many of our neighbors only pruned every other year because the heavier prunings were useful in the kitchen stove. They used a saw as well as snips. Now most families cook with gas so most of them prune every year as they don't need the wood. Coincidentally they find the yield is better and more even.

It is not a disaster if , once you've got the shape into your trees, you leave them unpruned in an occasional year. This would certainly be be an advantage to hobby farmers or those who have olives in their back garden. If you are taking the Big Trip OS for some months during the European summer you need not worry. Worry about the cat or dog, but not about leaving the olives unattended. Simply skip the pruning and do it a little harder the next year.

Pruning the tree

After we had cut back the bushy remnants of our old trees to three or four stems the next stage was to hollow out the centre. It seemed logical to us that picking would be easier if the crop was all around the outside and we did not have to scramble through the centre to grab the odd olive. We became more confident and started trimming up the trunks as we would have done with our vines and almond trees in the Barossa. Fortunately a neighbor, who had share farmed our grove for years before we purchased it, passed by and we asked for his comments. We were bought down to earth with his question "Why are you taking off all the best fruiting wood?" He went on to explain that cleaning out the centre was fine but that he would have left all the straggly bits around the outside. We took a closer look at the trees of our neighbors, and saw that their wine glasses had skirts. These skirts of straggly hanging growth produce good crops that are easily accessible for picking. Fortunately our over-enthusiastic pruning only damaged a couple of trees.

While many of our trees had reverted to a bush shape, we had another line of trees that had resisted the great frost of '85 better but were still overgrown. These trees are a local variety chosen for their strength and resistance. They have a massive trunk compared to other varieties and a heavy canopy and in the years of their abandonment they had become too high and extremely bushy. They bear a heavy crop and some of our worst picking in that first year was the result of being battered by the almost impenetrable interiors of these trees. They had grown to a height where picking could only be carried out with long ladders. The dense mass of unpruned growth in the centre had shaded out the lower part of the trees which were full of dead twigs.

Our first job was to ruthlessly reduce the height by about a half and then to restore the hollow centre. When this was done we found picking easier and the crop became much heavier and more reliable.

Optional tree shapes

Our major surgery had produced the two classic shapes for olive trees in central Italy (the wine glass and the multi-stemmed bowl) but other countries and other growers use different shapes for their particular purposes. Most of them look like the Italian wine glass but there are subtle differences.

The Spanish and Tunisian tree shape is useful in agro-olive plantations or alley planting. The trees have two limbs branching out from the central trunk instead of the three or four that form the wine glass. If these two are aligned with the row the effect is that of a trellised olive but without a trellis. The land can be worked and pasture can be planted and cut under the trees without the need for off-set machinery.

Then there is the mono-conical tree which has a central stem so that it develops a pyramidal shape like a Christmas tree. The fruiting branches hang down off the main central trunk. This shape has been developed in recent years because it was thought that the mono-conical tree would be better for mechanical picking when using shaker machines. The shaker machine sends a strong force up the single trunk and then travels out to the fruiting branches

---

FACING PAGE: *Detail of an olive branch. The fruiting wood will become exhausted and will be cut off. The shoots above will replace it and will be cut off in their turn.*

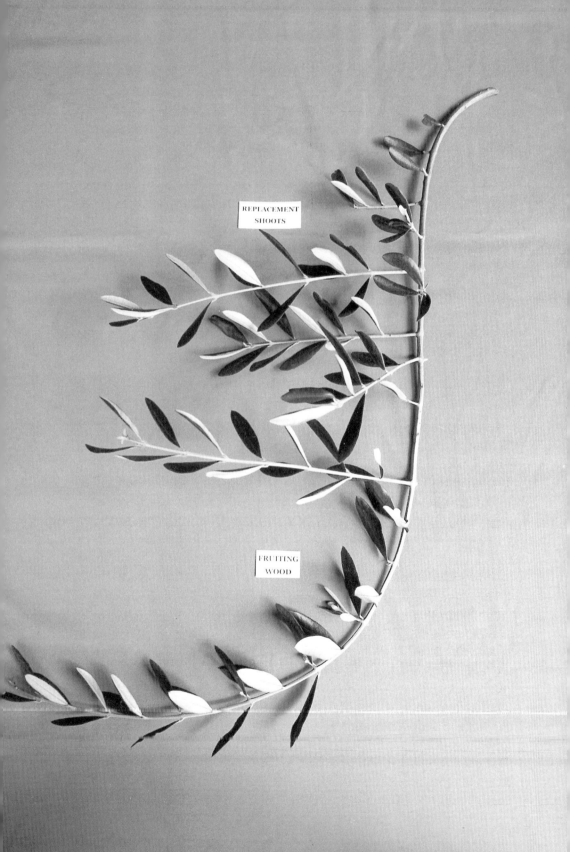

to make the fruit fall. It was thought that the single trunk would transmit the force of the shaker more efficiently. Some of the groves in Umbria have been pruned in this mono-conical form. The University at Perugia has carried out some comparative trials on mature trees and found that there is virtually no difference in the efficiency of machine picking when applied to either the mono-conical or the wine glass shape tree. If anything the wine glass is fractionally more efficient.

If the mono-conical tree is no better for machine picking it is certainly worse for hand picking or semi-mechanical picking and also for pruning. The problem is that as the tree grows it can only go up. The mono-conical tree gets taller quicker than a wine glass tree which has room to grow out as well as up. This means more ladder work and taller ladders.

To prune or not to prune

In the New world there is some discussion about whether trees would bear better if they were not pruned.

In Umbria and all of Italy the commercial plantings of olives are always pruned. There is no debate. The same applies to the other Mediterranean regions.

We certainly had a significant increase in yield after pruning our trees. Our yield increased from 6.5 kg of oil in 1992 to 22 kg in 1993 and then to 42 kg in 1994. A few years later we bought another two hectares of land which included more olive trees which we had to clear and restore. Our total yield then became 122 kg of oil but we estimated that our yield from the "old" block remained the same. Since the 1997 crop we have been recovering from a severe frost (not as bad as '85 but pretty bad) so yields have been lower. This increase in yield was not solely due to pruning as we had also applied fertiliser - the first ever on our trees as far as we knew. Fertiliser applications have continued but we believe that that first incremental leap was mainly due to the pruning.

There was debate in the journals in New Zealand a few years ago about whether to prune olive trees or not. Advice was given to growers to leave the trees for the first three years before pruning and then only to prune lightly. The growers there told us that they had been advised against heavy pruning of young trees because it weakens their growth and delays cropping.

Some of the trees we saw in New Zealand had not been seriously pruned for ten years and were taller than fifty year old trees in Umbria. The dense shade thrown by the thicket of twigs and branches severely reduced the crop on the lower part of the tree. The best crop was produced on the upper part of the tree. Pickers had to climb tall ladders to collect the total crop. The problem was exacerbated because much of the nursery stock they were buying was of poor quality and had not been shaped. When irrigation and fertilisers were applied to these young trees the result was often a thick untidy bush hardly recognisable as an olive tree. New Zealand nurseries have now greatly improved their stock and attention is paid to the important aspect of form. Growers are now being advised to prune their trees to retain a practical shape and allow ease of picking.

In Australia between 1850 and 1950 there were several attempts to establish an olive industry. These old trees still survive. They were initially well pruned but in spite of this example there are Australian growers who feel daunted at the thought of turning "natural" olive bushes into well shaped trees. If the same logic were applied to vines they would grow into tangled heaps on the ground. Other growers are pruning but seem unsure about the principles that underlie the logic of the process.

There has been some research in Italy into "non-pruning". After the great frost of 1985 killed all the above ground growth of many trees, a research centre in southern Tuscany decided to observe the effect of leaving unpruned the regrowth from the stump. When this regrowth became too tall and thick to be managed, they cut it off and allowed it to regrow. They still need to go through a number of cycles to determine an average yield and to see whether the yield reduction caused by total removal of the top part of the tree is off-set by higher yields at other parts of the cycle, or by reduced pruning costs. There has not been any commercial adoption of the idea.

The reason for pruning

At every stage of the fruits' development, from the initiation of the bud to the mature fruit, sunlight is required. Small fruiting wood will die in the dense shade of unpruned trees. Old trees that have not been pruned for years are full of dead wood. Pruning is also important for hand picking and when using a semi-mechanical picker with wands. Tall trees need a lot of ladder work. A high concentration of tangled shoots makes it difficult to pick. There are big improvements in efficiency if the fruit is clustered together and clearly visible on the outside of the trees.

Picking is the major bottleneck and the major cost in olive production. While the yield increase we obtained from pruning was most rewarding the increased efficiency of picking was just as important. Our yield increase has been achieved at the same time as our trees have become smaller. The actual time spent picking has increased only slightly in relation to the extra yield.

The productivity of the labor involved has probably increased three or four times. When you pick a well pruned tree the fruits are dense on the branches and one strips them off in great showers. With an unpruned tree it is time consuming to search for the sparse fruit.

Olives are notorious biennial croppers. The district statistics for Italian olive growing regions clearly demonstrate this biennial cropping pattern. It is claimed that good pruning will even out the yield from year to year. This claim has limited validity. The trees still have good and bad years but pruning ensures that the bad years are better. With unpruned trees the production in the off year can be zero. To start with our trees were out of phase with each other so the good and bad crops in different parts of the grove balanced each other. Now we have had a severe frost that has damaged all the trees to some degree and we will probably have a good and bad year pattern for the grove as a whole. It is not yet possible to control the biennial pattern and we have to factor this into our expectations of yield.

Maintenance pruning

Once we had restored our trees from years of neglect we found that we had a sucker problem for a few years. The vigour of the tree has to go somewhere and while there were a large number of shoots on the top part of the tree there were a large number of suckers from the stump. Following any severe check in growth (pruning or frost) dormant buds on the trunk tend to shoot out. Most of these shoots can be cleaned off but where they occur more than a metre up the trunk they can be used to restore the "skirt" that has been lost due to shading. After a few years of careful pruning our trees were back in balance and the sucker problem is greatly reduced.

Maintenance pruning introduced different decisions which we found difficult to sort out. We thought it was just our unfamiliarity with olives but the Professor from Perugia who conducted our olive management course confirmed that even people who have spent their lives with olives have moments of uncertainty. Local olive growers who do their own pruning usually bring in a professional "gun" pruner every three or four years to keep their trees in shape.

During the pruning section of the course we were taught to recognise three types of wood based on direction of growth.

(a) There is the **vertical** growth which produces little fruit. This seems to be a natural direction for the tree to grow and many growers are doubtful of interfering with this. Yet most of the verticals must be removed. A few need to be left to provide further lateral shoots in future years. Even these must be checked in a particular fashion. Each single vertical that is left has to be trained to grow year after year in a upward but zig zag direction. Each year the upward growth is pruned so that a lateral will emerge to provide the upward direction for the following year.

(b) There are the **horizontal or 45°** degree angled shoots. These are good fruiting wood and are left unpruned.

(c) Finally there is the growth that **hangs down** below the horizontal. This was probably horizontal the year before and has sagged under the weight of the crop. This needs to be trimmed or thinned out carefully but not completely removed as it is good fruiting wood. When it has become exhausted from heavy cropping over time and full of dead twigs it is time to remove it.

In general maintenance pruning consists of taking out the excess verticals and cleaning up the exhausted fruiting wood. From time to time we have to make some big cuts to stop the trees from getting too tall or too wide. New shoots are forced out of the dormant buds and we can start pruning for laterals and downward growth again.

Pruning for quality

If you are familiar with vines you will know that many growers deliberately reduce the yield of their vines in order to enhance the quality of their grapes. There is a tradeoff between yield and quality with vines. If the yield is high, the quality is low, and if the yield is reduced the quality increases. We know of no attempt by olive growers to reduce the yield deliberately through regular severe pruning in order to improve the quality of the oil. That is not to say that yield and quality are not related.

Generally growers rely on good pruning to enhance the quality that is initially determined by climatic factors. Good pruning allows sufficient light to penetrate the tree. Experiments with artificial shading of trees have shown that shaded fruit does not develop flavor as well as fruit that is exposed to direct sunlight. Direct sunlight also favors the production of the oil content of the fruit so good pruning will increase both oil yield and flavor.

How much do you prune?

We absorbed all the available information we could find about the results that could be obtained by good pruning, but each year confronted us with the conundrum. How do you know when you have taken off enough? With vines you can prune to various levels by leaving different numbers of buds but no such easy formula has been found for olive trees. The difficulty can be summed up by the following verse:

Big fleas have little fleas upon their backs to bite 'em
Little fleas have smaller fleas and so ad infinitum.

We found that we could recognise the different types of wood but then each class of wood had the other classes of wood on it and so .... ad infinitum. The question was how far down the branch do you go? We asked the President of the Mount Amiata Olive Growers Association, who thought for a while, and then replied "Until you run out of patience."

We later came upon another old Umbrian saying that you should prune the olive trees until they are open enough for the birds to fly through them.

As latter-day Australians we privately thought there must be a more scientific method of determining the optimum "pruning level".

It became a high priority to put this question during the olive management course.

The first scientific response we got was that of the Leaf Area Index. This involves counting all the leaves on the tree, and replaced the idea of watching birds. It sounds a good cure for pruners' insomnia but as a serious guide to pruning we wondered if it was be one of those jokes Italians play on naive foreigners. The equivalent of the crows flying backwards in the Mallee to keep the sand out of their eyes. As it turned out, the Leaf Area Index can be a serious tool for those learning to prune.

Each leaf on the tree requires some direct sunlight on it during some part of the day. Scientists have worked out that a Leaf Area Index of between 3 and 4 is ideal for the penetration of sunlight into the olive. To obtain the Leaf Area Index one multiplies the total number of leaves on the tree by their average area. This is then divided by the area covered by the tree.

$$\frac{\text{Number of leaves X Average area of each leaf}}{\text{Area covered by tree}}$$

A Leaf Area Index of 3 means that there are three leaves covering each piece of land under the tree. With a Leaf Area Index of 4 there are four leaves and so on. The higher the Index the more leaves over each piece of land and the more interception of light.

FACING PAGE: **A beautiful old wine glass olive tree near Orvieto. Note the skirt of fruiting wood and the upward growth formed from zig zags over many years.**

The crucial measurement is the light penetration which can be taken simply with the light meter used by professional photographers. A comparison between the direct reading outside the tree and the reading in the shade will give you the Leaf Area Index. All you need is the assistance of a tame technician from a research centre to assist you in calibrating the relationship between meter readings and the leaf area index. Alternatively if you take one of the many olive study tours to Italy and Spain you could calibrate your light meter against well pruned trees in those countries. As far as we know there are no "Prunometers" on the market yet but the principal is simple and you heard about it here first.

We were a bit abashed by all this high falutin' exactitude and were relieved to find that there are several other indicators that are more to the taste of a simple farmer.

Under-pruning can creep up on the olive grower. You don't want to wait until the body of the tree is showing a lot of dead twigs. One early indicator of incipient under-pruning is a change to the straggly fruiting wood in the skirt. If the wood has grown long and particularly straggly and has sparse leaves of a darker green than normal on the tips, then action needs to be taken to reduce the shade by heavier pruning higher up the tree. In addition, over shading will be indicated when there are few new horizontal or 45° angle shoots. This is another sure sign that more thinning is required above the skirt.

Another indicator of the adequacy of the pruning is the length of the shoots from the previous year. With an unpruned or very lightly pruned tree these new shoots will on average be about 2 to 5 cm long. In the following year when they become fruiting wood they will produce perhaps one olive and as these shoots are scattered the fruit will be difficult to pick.

A well pruned tree will produce new shoots of about 20 to 40 cm in length. Fruit will hang in clusters and can be harvested more efficiently.

If the tree has been too severely pruned - for example when you are knocking an old tree back into shape - the shoots will be 50 cm or more in length. These shoots have passed the optimum ratio of fruit to vegetative growth, and although the yield probably won't suffer in the initial year, it will be necessary in the following year to prune less severely to encourage a return to medium length shoots.

Balanced pruning

One of the objectives of pruning is to balance next year's growth against this year's crop. It is the competition from unpruned trees for water and nutrients for both this year's crop and next year's crop that causes the wild fluctuations in yield. In September buds are formed that will become flowers and fruit in the following year. At the same time the small olives on the tree are beginning to grow rapidly and produce oil in their pulp. If there is a heavy crop of fruit next year's buds will be starved of nutrients. If there is a light crop there will be a large surplus for the buds. Good pruning will enable these demands to be balanced as much as possible, but of course, seasonal conditions will have an effect on yield as well. Experience has shown that well pruned trees show less tendency to extreme fluctuations even in harsh climatic conditions than those that are unpruned.

Mechanical pruning

There are various approaches that are being looked at based on machines that go down the rows "mowing" the trees but most are little more than a gleam in the eye of the inventor. There are some mechanical aids available for hand pruning such as pneumatic snips and chain saws and these can be helpful.

Disposal of the prunings

It was thought that burning the olive tree prunings controlled some pests and diseases. In fact Mussolini, in one of his many attempts to manage Italian agriculture through legislation, passed a law to make burning compulsory.

Many Italian experts now recommend that prunings be chopped and left on the ground to rot but in spite of this, and the contribution the smoke makes to pollution, burning remains the most popular method of disposal.

If the land between the trees is cultivated every year for weed control then returning the finely chopped prunings to the soil as organic matter is valuable.

If the land between is under pasture the need for additional organic matter is not so great.

Because we encouraged pasture between our trees we used to remove and then burn all our prunings but since we bought our Lamborghini tractor and trinciatore we have been chopping them up and leaving them on the pasture. The trinciatore is a machine similar to a forage harvester with flails that chop the prunings finely and leave them on the ground. We haven't tried to use a tandem disc for this purpose as we used to find in Australia that prunings of this type will only block the disc and a great deal of time will be wasted to little purpose. If a machine to chop the prunings finely is not on hand then summer barbecues and winter kindling are better ways of burning olive wood than setting fire to a heap of it in a field.

We've thought about letting sheep in to eat the leaves on the pruned branches, but as they are produced in winter they don't have much value and there is plenty of more palatable pasture around and about.

Olive wood is of high quality but the size of the prunings are generally so small that it is difficult to find uses for it. Some local artigiani (craftsmen) turn it into wooden spoons and other small objects, but there is a limit to the number of wooden spoons we can use in our kitchen, and neither of us is much of a dab hand at carving. The really important olive wood for carving is that from old trees when they are cut back because they are too tall or when they must be removed because of extensive frost damage. This wood is used for stools, bowls, benches and other attractive rustic objects. Local carvers are always keen to acquire this type of wood and we have several lovely bowls and plates that we use regularly.

Chapter 6

PICKING FOR FLAVOR AND QUALITY

The olive harvest

The olive harvest is a dream compared to the grape harvest. It is so relaxing not having to worry about the rain, the sugar content and the dozens of other problems that beset more perishable crops. Admittedly we are hobby farmers and not dependent on olives for our livelihood but our neighbors, who have been involved with olives all their lives, say that olives are rarely struck by disaster at harvest. We have plenty of other weather events that can destroy the crop in the developing stages - frost and hail in particular - but harvesting is peaceful.

Judging the time for harvesting

We harvest our olives in November which is the end of autumn here and a month after the grape vintage. Tradition dictates that we start picking here on St Catherine's day which is 25th November but this tradition is frequently broken and we are usually well into the harvest by the 15th November. We used to worry about the St. Catherine's date as it seemed very late, and eventually we found that it is better to pick about 10 days earlier than this if we want to get better oil. The reasons that convinced us came initially from the olive courses we attended and then from the results we obtained. Most growers in our neighborhood are picking earlier now and some even begin before we do. The factors to take into account when deciding when to pick are:

(a) *oil yield*

Growers do not test their olives for oil percentage before picking, unlike grapes where growers usually measure the level of sugar before picking can start. In our zone the percentage of oil is different every year due to climatic variations.

Nonetheless growers in the past tried to pick at the time when the oil yield is at its best. Research shows that the oil production in the fruit increases rapidly from early September through until the end of October. The temperature in our zone then drops as we move into winter and the oil percentage increases slightly for another two or three weeks - roughly St Catherine's day. After that date there continues to be a slight increase in the percentage of oil but it is simply that the fruit dehydrates and, in fact, the yield of oil remains the same.

Old farmers have told us that when the harvest took much longer in the past because of the slow processing at the mill, olives were sometimes not picked until January by which time the oil content of the fruit was very high indeed. When they compared their results with others who had milled earlier there was little if any difference in the total yield of oil because the weight of the fresh olives was much less due to dehydration.

If you decide you want a particular "target percentage" of oil you can usually achieve it if you wait long enough, but it will be through water loss rather than any real increase in oil yield.

St Catherine's day, 25th November, is probably the date when the maximum oil yield is achieved in this district but most growers find that although an earlier picking will yield a little less, the quality of the oil is better because they pick more green fruit.

One needs to be cautious about interpreting the local folk law because of the changing objectives of olive oil production. In the past farmers depended on the oil for their own use. Their wish to obtain the maximum yield of oil combined with the slow rate of pressing at the mill all encouraged later picking. Now there is a greater awareness of the need to pick early to obtain better flavor and color.

(b) color

You cannot rely on the color of the olive to determine the optimum harvest time either. In our zone it is normal for some of the olives to be green, or at least mauve, rather than black at harvest. The color of the fruit of some varieties is almost completely green at harvest. For example *Leccino,* one of the classic varieties of central Italy, is usually black when picked but *Frantoio* (another classic in our zone) has mostly green fruit. The famous Roman agricultural writer, M.P. Catone (234 to 149 BC) states *"Quam acerbissima olea oleum facies, tam oleum optimum erit"* or *'the more green olives there are the better the quality of the oil'.*

(c) fruit fall

We can eliminate oil percentage and color as means of determining the optimum time of harvest but research shows that "fruit fall" is the most useful method of determining the harvest date. As the calender date of fruit fall is remarkably stable year after year it is reasonable to use a fixed date for the olive harvest. It may vary a few days from year to year but is remarkably stable thus allowing a degree of certainty about the picking date.

Fruit fall in our zone begins about the middle of November and continues to increase week by week until about 6 to 8 % of the olives have fallen by 15th December. The rate of fruit fall rises week by week exponentially and will become a serious economic loss if picking is delayed beyond this point. After the 15th December another week may see fruit fall double to 12 to 16% and another week's delay results in another doubling. Obviously these losses are unacceptable so our local advisers recommend that we start about a month before 15th December, that is on 15th November. Once the fruit fall pattern has been measured the date for harvest can be set with rarely a few days variation from year to year.

Picking for flavor

Earlier picking is better for quality as the polyphenol level, which is one of the most important flavor elements, declines once the fruit is mature. Fruit that is picked in the earlier part of the harvest period will produce stronger flavored and more peppery oil.

This does vary according to the variety of the trees. "Early maturing" varieties in our zone are those that lose their polyphenol level quickly (such as *Leccino*). These must be picked early for a quality oil.

"Late maturing" varieties are those that hold polyphenol levels better (such as *Frantoio* and *Moraiolo*) and they can be picked later in the harvest period without sacrificing quality. This is only a matter of a few weeks as really late harvesting will see a sharp decline in quality in all varieties.

Another indicator of flavor is the color of the pulp. When the fruit is fully mature the pulp as well as the skin will be colored and the flavor of the oil will be bland.

If fruit were picked earlier than the end of October would oil yields fall substantially? Polyphenols levels would be higher but other flavor components would not necessarily have developed. The oil might be more peppery but could be lacking in fruit and balance. If the fruit were picked early the oil yield would be lower but would probably not lose more than 1%.

Time for machine picking

Mechanical picking using a shaker works best when the fruit is fully mature and fruit fall is imminent. Mechanical picking using the shaker is difficult to combine with quality oil production. The machine needs to shake most of the fruit from the tree if it is to be an economical operation and this means that the fruit must not be too firmly attached to the branch. The best time to pick for flavor is while the fruit is still slightly immature, that is, before excessive fruit fall, and at this stage it is very firmly attached to the branch.

This was demonstrated at our harvesting field day. We had already picked more than half our olives on our own grove by 20th November when the the field day was held. The instructor warned us the results would not be good as his measurement with the "pull" meter showed that the fruits were still strongly attached to the tree. The shaker was bought into action and the remainder were handpicked to measure efficiency. The shaker took off 75% of the crop and the instructor estimated that another week would be needed to reach an acceptable 90% level. This would mean picking on 27th November which is the second half of the harvest period when flavors are declining rapidly. If one picks really late with a mechanical harvester the efficiency may be high in terms of the percentage of fruit gathered from the tree but if the fruit has started to fall in large quantities the overall yield of oil will be reduced.

Mechanical pickers using wands do work well in the early harvest period and can be used for quality oil production but their output is much lower than the tree shaker.

Picking in the rain

Rain does not rot the olives as it does grapes and other fruit but picking in the rain is not a good thing to do. When the olives go to the mill the first operation is washing and blowing out the leaves but don't be tempted to pick olives when they are wet - especially if the harvest is running late. You would need to be desperate as hand picking wet trees is a miserable job. A wet suit is the minimum requirement.

Fortunately there are some sound reasons for not picking wet olives. Wet olives will go mouldy during storage. This is death to quality. Bacterial diseases are transmitted by rain and can infect the tree through scrapes and abrasions caused to the twigs and branches during picking.

Hand picking

Hand picking is always slow but picking individual olives on poorly pruned and uncared for trees is a hopeless task.The olives on well pruned trees are in dense clusters instead of ones and twos. The technique is to strip the clusters through the fingers so the olives fall off in great showers. In our area of Umbria hand harvesting is almost universal.

(a) *The net*

The most important piece of harvesting equipment is the net. Nets are now made from nylon and the mesh is designed to catch the olives but not let them through. The correct net prevents the olives bouncing and rolling as they do on solid material. Of course if the slope is very steep they will roll off and it is necessary to prop up the lower side. The net is made of two long pieces sewn together half way along the middle seam. This means that one half is on one side of the tree, the other on the other side and there is only a short part that needs to be overlapped and held with stones or clips. It is worth taking trouble over the placing of the net as picking olives is slow work and you don't want to lose a single one.

There will inevitably be quite a lot of leaves mixed with the olives on the net - particularly if you use a small rake as a harvesting aid. While they are on the net remove any leaves that are attached to olives but otherwise don't worry too much as these are easily removed at the mill.

You should get a net that is the right size for your trees as it is pointless dragging around a huge net for small trees. Here in Italy they come in three sizes from 5X5 to 8X8 metres. The 8X8 net cost about $ 60.

A tip for the hobby farmer or garden producer is to put the nets into black plastic bags when storing them. They are made of a nylon material which breaks down in sunlight. For the small producer the net should last for ever if it is not exposed to sunlight during storage and there should be little damage to the net from snags when only a few trees are picked.

(b) *Ladders*

As well as the net you will needs some ladders as the trees become taller. Normally the ladders, made from chestnut wood are leant against the trees but we have found that an aluminium step ladder is also useful.

(c) *Gloves and rake and a basket*

Gloves are essential - particularly if it is very cold. A small hand-held rake can be a help in stripping the fruit off the branch and many of our neighbors use those. They are very effective when the olives are thick and on downward hanging branches. In Tunisia they use plastic finger extensions to strip the fruit. A basket that straps around the waist is a useful piece of equipment for really small trees where the crop is so light that it is not worth putting down the net. The basket is curved, fits comfortably around the waist and is held with a strap. It leaves both hands free for picking.

Semi-Mechanical picking

Semi-mechanical picking is now becoming more widely adopted and could take over from hand picking on most large groves in a few years. We have some neighbors who have bought a machine for their medium sized grove.

The best machine is driven by compressed air. There is a wand with a small air motor which drives a number of fingers in the form of a comb or rake that move backwards and forwards. The net is place on the ground in the same way as when hand picking. The picking action is to drag the comb through the tree. The comb does not have to come in contact with the olive to knock it off. The beating action of the comb on the small wood shakes off the olives. As the force is applied close to the olive they are dislodged even if the picking is early and the attachment force is still strong. Any olives that are not dislodged by shaking the wood are knocked off by direct contact with the moving comb. One wand is long enough to reach the top of the tree without using ladders. The other wand is short for the lower part of the tree. The unit needs a motor (or the PTO of a tractor) and compressor to provide the air. The cost is about $3,000 for a compressor and two wands. Normally there are two operators to work the wands.

The growers we know who have this machine and speak very highly of it. We have seen it in operation and it is certainly very effective in getting the olives off the tree. One friend has a grove 100 metres higher than ours at 650 metres above sea level so many of the olives are tough to get off at harvest time. He works the machine with a team of four. Two people operate the wands and two move the nets. Picking rates are difficult to estimate as the time taken is the same whether there is a heavy crop or a light one. He says that 400 to 800 kg per day for the team or double the rate of good hand picking is a reasonable guess. The best arrangement is for the operators to change with the net gatherers as working the wands is hard work.

At a recent field day we saw another picking aid. It was similar to the air driven wand but was powered by a 12 v electric motor. The electric supply is taken from a tractor or ute. The action is different as the fingers of the comb do not beat back and forth but are rotated. The wavy fingers rotate and agitate the area of the tree they are in contact with and dislodge the fruit. The electric wand is only new and at this stage is not nearly as effective as the air driven machine. The main advantage is the cost is lower for the very small grower. A single wand costs about $1200 whereas the air driven unit is $3000 but as there are two wands it is only $1500 per operator which is hardly anything extra for a much more effective machine.

Fully Mechanical picking

There are two forms of fully mechanical picking. There is a larger version of the beating fingers and there is the tree shaker. We have not seen the tractor mounted beaters being used on olive groves in this zone but the trials indicate that they should be quite effective. As they are able to dislodge fruit early in the picking season they would be compatible with the production of quality oil.

The beater fingers come in all shapes and sizes but essentially they are based on the same principal as the air-driven hand-held wands. As they are much larger and heavier they are moved round the tree using an articulated arm mounted on the back of a tractor - a lighter version of a back hoe arm.

The tree shaker locks on to the trunk of the tree and removes the fruit by vibration. The original models required a large tractor of 100 to 120 HP as weight was most important. The machine shook the tree against the inertia of the tractor. The new models are mounted on a front end loader of a medium sized tractor of about 60 HP. Because the shaking mechanism is hung loose from the loader with chains the inertia of the tractor is not important.

After considerable research into the rival merits of various shaking actions the latest machines now have a cycle of orbital vibration that twists the fruit round and round followed by a cycle of multi directional vibration that swings the fruit back and forth. If one circuit does not get them the other should.

The shaker cannot be used on small trees or very large ones. In Italy it is considered unwise to use it on trees with trunks less than 7 to 8 cm in diameter or 8 years old and usually trees that have trunks over 40 to 50 cm or 60 years old are too solid to shake properly. In central Italy there are millions of trees that have been frosted off at various times and have regrown in the form of multi stem trees. The shaker head is too cumbersome to use on this type of tree and can cause considerable damage as the suckers are not always well attached to the old stump and can break off when shaken. It is recognised that small fruit of less than 1.5 gm are mostly left on the tree when a shaker is used. It is important , if you want to use these machines, to plant varieties that have large fruit for efficient harvesting.

The shaker machines cost about $20,000 to $30,000 each.

Nets for mechanical picking

It is necessary to use larger and stronger nets when mechanically picking as the tractors will operate on them. The mechanical picking methods (both fully and semi) all throw the fruit considerable distances so the nets also need to be larger than those used for hand picking. At the demonstration held in our village they used long lengths of a plastic shade cloth material.

While the tree shaker method of picking is extremely quick, the bottleneck becomes the setting and gathering of the nets.

A mechanised net is available in the form of an inverted umbrella. It is attached to the jaws of the shaker and as they move round the trunk the catching umbrella closes round as well. The fruit is shaken off into the umbrella and rolls down to a trough behind the jaws. While this machine is the ultimate in mechanical picking of olive trees it is not the most effective as the umbrella touches the lower part of the tree and nullifies the vibration. This reduces the efficiency of harvesting.

There is an intermediate system between the hand operated nets and the umbrella which is quite popular in the south of Italy where shakers are widely used. The nets are spread by hand from a trailer and then wound back in with a power driven reel with the olives feeding directly into a trailer.

Rates of picking olives

One of the first things we learnt with our olive grove is that there is no uniform "picking rate" for olives. It depends on the trees, the crop, the pruning, the terrain and of course the skill of the operators. It is easy to undervalue hand picking skills as it seems so easy to grab a few olives but to pick at a good rate requires years of practice. We have improved our picking skills over the years but still come well behind our neighbors who have done it for decades. Even the best "gun" picker can be foiled by a poor crop. We have seen some of our best local pickers get a miserable half bucket of olives in a couple of hours off poor trees. If you can pick 8 to 10 kg of fresh olives per hour by hand you are doing well.

To compare the rates achieved with different methods of mechanical picking is extremely difficult as each one has its advantages and disadvantages.

In one trial carried out late in the harvest period the four main methods were compared. All achieved over 90% harvest efficiency and all used hand operated nets to keep the comparison simple.

Hand picking managed 8 to 10 kg per person per hour. This rate doubled when air-driven hand-held beaters were used. Tractor mounted large beaters doubled it again and the shaker doubled it yet again.

From 10 kg per person per hour to 90 kg per person per hour were the results from this trial.

While the actual quantity depends on the crop the ratios between the various systems appear to be similar in many trials but remember these have been conducted late in the harvest period to reduce the variables.

If you pick early the high rate for the shaker would have to be offset against a lower efficiency. The unpicked olives would either be wasted or, as on some olive groves in the south of Italy, a team of gleaners would have to be employed to recover them.

The use of the inverted umbrella form of net with the shaker again doubles the rate per picker but the efficiency of harvesting is 5 to 10% lower depending on how much of the "skirt" of the tree is in contact with the umbrella.

The great thing about handpicked olives is that the label "handpicked, organically grown" can add quite a bit to the price in a boutique shop.

Collateral damage when picking

Mechanical harvesting causes damage to the fruit, to the small branches, and results in a loss of leaves.

The damage to the fruit from hand picking is slight. It is increased when using beaters but this should not cause any significant reduction in quality provided the fruit is taken for processing quickly.

The small branches are damaged by abrasion when either of the two types of beaters are used. The large tractor mounted machines do more damage than the hand held beaters. These abrasions could be an entry point for bacterial diseases which enter the tree through damaged bark and there is some talk of spraying the trees after this method of picking with a copper spray to protect them.

Leaf loss is not considered serious below about 10% but the tractor mounted beater can at times come close to this figure.

Choosing the best method of picking

Obviously every method has its problems.

Hand harvesting is costly. We could not afford to pay for hand picking on wages. If pickers harvested 8 kg hour and we got 16% oil we would have 1.3 kg of oil per hour. We sell our oil retail but the wholesale price is around $13 to $15 a kg which would give us a return of about $16.50 an hour. The average wage for farm work is about $15 an hour so we would be left with $1.50 to cover all our other costs. Processing the oil at the frantoio will cost $1.50 a kg so the return would be zero and we would have to bear the costs of cultivation, fertiliser, transport, equipment and our own time.

The air driven beaters double picking rates and are not a large capital outlay. When our young trees are in production we will get one of these machines. This will enable us to take our crop off ourselves and make us less dependent on outside labor.

The tractor mounted beaters double output again but are a large capital outlay. They cause damage to the small branches and considerable leaf loss. We wouldn't be able to justify this investment, but a medium sized commercial producer may find it useful.

The shaker appears to be the most productive system but some of that productivity is an illusion. The efficiency is low early in the harvest period when the fruit is strongly attached. The harvesting may be cheap but there are high opportunity costs if only 75% of the fruit is recovered. If harvesting is prolonged there is a natural fall of fruit. Low harvesting costs have to be offset again by a failure to harvest all the crop. The shaker has limited value for the production of quality oils as these need to be picked early. The shaker with an umbrella attachment is the most productive system for labor efficiency but harvests less fruit. We would not even consider this method, but a large commercial producer may well do so.

Handling the olives after picking by hand

For the first five years of our olive venture we picked our olives into buckets, bins and bags and took them down to the padrone's garage where we emptied them into his large storage trays. These are nearly a metre long and half a metre wide and 20 cm deep. The olives are spread in these trays and the trays stacked so the air circulates between them. All the pickers had their separate stacks.

When the picking was finished our padrone would preside, in the presence of all the pickers, while the trays were emptied down a riddle to remove some of the leaves. They were then scooped into sacks. These sacks were solemnly weighed and the shares recorded in the padrone's book. Most of the olives came from the padrone's grove but were picked by different pickers. One stack of trays would be weighed in as Padrone 50% and Giovanni 50% while the next stack would be one Giovanni picked with his son Renato and his family so this lot would be marked down as 50:25:25. Then olives from grove owners such as ourselves would be allocated 100% to us .

The olives were packed into second hand Hessian coffee sacks that had been collected from the olive mill - the frantoio - and at first we wondered if these sacks revealed some secret process for the production of quality oil. Whisky, for instance, is matured in old sherry casks to achieve a special aroma.

We rather disappointingly found that it was due to the fact that there was a large coffee blender in the nearby town and a lot a cheap second hand sacks were available.

After the weighing ceremony a time would be booked at the frantoio, usually some unearthly hour in the early morning, and the truck load of sacks would be taken to the frantoio and weighed in total on their more modern scales. After the olives had been crushed, the padrone calculated the percentage of oil and distributed it and the processing charges to each participant in the proportions previously decided .

This is the traditional method of handling the olives and dates back to mediaeval times and the days of share farming.

Now, having taken part in various olive extension courses, we realise that there are better ways of retaining oil quality. The fact that the padrone's oil was excellent is remarkable proof of the "surplus" of flavor that we produce in this zone. For the last two or three years we have moved our olives directly from the nets into plastic mesh crates - not sacks or solid bins - and stacked them in a cool shed. We try to avoid moving them about from crate to crate and do not put them into sacks for the journey to the frantoio. Eight years ago most of the olives coming into the frantoio were in sacks which were often stacked too deep and the oil oozed out from the bruised olives at the bottom. Now more and more growers are moving over to crates and the quality of the olives is much better.

Whereas our padrone waited until the harvest was finished before taking all the olives to the frantoio we take ours in batches every four days. The rough rule of thumb is that olives lose about half their flavor components if they are stored a week and 80% if they are stored for two weeks. We get our olives to the frantoio on an average of two days which is quite reasonable in cool weather. We cannot take them to the frantoio more frequently as the millowner does not like processing very small lots of olives and prefers at least 200 kg. We would also lose a lot of time as the journey to the frantoio takes about half an hour and we would have to wait for our turn in the queue to have the olives pressed.

Our local technical advisers are trying to persuade the growers, so far with little success, to bulk their olives with their neighbors and process them more frequently for the sake of quality. The growers respond by saying they do not want to mix their magnificent olives with the poxy ones produced by the grower down the road but the advisers claim that it is one of those win-win sums we are all looking for. Even if the neighbor with the "poxy" olives does get better oil from the blend everyone's oil is better from the rapid processing.

Handling mechanically picked olives

With fully mechanical harvesting the problem of waiting to bulk up should not arise as the rapid rate of harvesting means that the grower will probably take the olives to the frantoio at least once a day. This is important as mechanically picked olives are almost identical in terms of quality when picked but deteriorate more rapidly when stored.

Chapter 7

BEES AROUND THE OLIVE MILL

The frantoio - the olive oil mill

To us, the sight of our beautiful green oil flowing from the frantoio tap into our jars is particularly satisfying. Most growers deliver their produce to factories where milk has to be pasteurised, grape juice is turned into wine, and most orange juice is blended and added to for shelf life. Along the way any idea that "our" fruit remains identifiable is lost. We small growers keep our eye on our olives from flower to oil - it is an intimacy rarely available to farmers these days. Olives are one of the few remaining products that can be turned into the end product, that is oil, without undergoing any chemical process and without any additive being needed to "make it last". You can put your finger into the oil as it emerges from the tap and taste it then and there. At our frantoio the owner's wife takes this very oil and makes great plates of bruschetta for all of us in the kitchen that is part of the frantoio. She has a fire burning in the fireplace at which we toast our toes when the wait is long and the day (or night) is cold, and her husband puts out jars of his rough home made wine with which to wash down the bruschetta.

Activity at the frantoio during the olive harvest brings a totally new meaning to "bees around a honey pot". "Bee" in Italian is "Ape" (pronounced "aapay"). It is the common name for a small three-wheeled transporter used by Italian farmers. In the 1950's and 60's the "Vespa" motorscooter - "wasp" in English - became a symbol of Italian youth. By the 1970's they had all been ridden off into the archives for classic films as Italian youth abandoned their scooters for cars but the Vespa's hard working cousin, the "Ape" continues to be produced and became the symbol of the small share farmer. The Ape is a scooter with a trailer and a tiny cab. It makes the same high whine and loud buzzing sound as its better known predecessor the Vespa. The Api (plural) are cursed by sophisticated Romans who try to drive the country roads with the same flare and daring as they do in the city. Share farmers, their wives bulked up along side in the little cab, toddle along at their own pace, totally impervious to the hoots and flashing headlights of the Alfa Romeo's and wall-to-wall carpeted four-by-fours beloved by weekend barones. The *Ape* has replaced the donkey but the slow country rhythm remains and they give way to no *arriviste* of a motor car.

At the frantoio the *Api* resemble bees around a honey pot as they cluster in the mill yard bearing the olive harvest of individual growers. The farmers leave them to check on their place in the queue, then drive them into the mill to unload the olives. When the oil is ready they load the *Ape* with the empty crates and the drums of fresh oil and whine and buzz off home.

They are not the only motors in the yard. There are the larger farmers' trucks, some tractors and trailers and, standing out among all the small farmers, one or two wealthy Romans dressed in their most fashionable "country" clothes and, as it's usually bitterly cold, their best fur coats. They swish up in their expensive cars to collect their share of the oil harvested from their hobby farm picked and worked by a neighboring small farmer.

The frantoio

We have many frantoio to choose from within a fifteen kilometre radius of our olive grove. In our early days our olives went to a nearby village where there was an old style frantoio but we saw nothing of the process as our olives went with those of our neighbors. When that frantoio closed down we had to make a choice from the other frantoio. The clerk of our local comune decided to set up a mill, and as a gesture of parochial loyalty, we opted for that.

His first year was a bit rocky. The established mills take a percentage of the oil from each grower to pay for the processing instead of cash. As he needed cash, he decided to take payment in cash only. The local farmers were outraged at this breaching of the exchange economy, and muttered about going elsewhere. However, the following year they all turned up and, like us, have settled down as old and valued clients. The mill owner is now able to take oil instead of cash, so everyone is happy.

The big change for us all was that the new frantoio was built with a centrifugal press instead of the old mat press. Again there were mutterings - it couldn't be possible to produce the best oil with newfangled machinery. But it did and does.

The process

We growers are in the hands of the frantoio when it comes to the ultimate quality of our oil and we decided it was worth trying to understand the extraction process to make sure we had made the right decision. After all, if the pressing isn't up to scratch, then wise growers vote with their olives and take them to another frantoio.

We began by investigating the mat-process story. The padrone of our village of San Pietro told us the real story before he died. In the old days the olives were taken to the old mat press frantoio which was so slow that the olives had to be stored for days or even weeks awaiting processing. The olives lost their flavor, they went mouldy (creating new "off" flavors), fermented, and some of the precious oil oozed out as the olives were often stacked a metre deep. On a visit to nearby Foligno in Umbria we saw a magnificent old frantoio with a huge upstairs storage barn where the olives had been stored awaiting processing. The windows were left open in a vain attempt to reduce mould and keep them fresh. The new processing machinery at this frantoio now processes more olives in an hour than the old presses did in a day. There is no backlog and the vast storage barn is now empty, but still admired and preserved for its superb architecture.

Some boutique producers still use the mat-press and these presses are available in mini form for hobby farmers. They will produce excellent oil provided the processing is rapid.

It is not enough just to get the olives to the frantoio as soon as possible after picking. To get the best quality oil out of the press there is also a need to shift the paste from the grinding wheels or the hammer mill to the baskets and into the press reasonably quickly and, once the oil and juice has been extracted, to separate the oil from the juice as soon as possible. The mat-press is fine if there is only a small quantity of olives to be processed. As soon as the throughput is slowed down, the resultant quality is compromised.

Earning your frantoio spurs

It was only after several years that the locals decided we were responsible enough to be included in the intimacy of life at the frantoio.

Our initial exclusion from the intimacy of the frantoio had its roots in the perception of local farmers who consider (privately) that all *stranieri* are unreliable and fly-by-night. They would never betray this to the *stranieri* (such discourtesy is not acceptable) but among themselves they consider that even the nicest *stranieri* come for the summer like the swallows, perhaps write articles or books about the glories of the Italian countryside and its lovable peasants, and then disappear in winter when the freezing Tramontana blows down from Siberia. They are eager to take part in a bucolic vintage in October but have gone by November when the tougher olive harvest is in full swing.

We did not disappear to Australia for a winter migration, but it took quite a few years before it was decided that we were responsible enough to actually go to the frantoio. Initially we were only allowed to be bag humpers in the padrone's garage. But the day came when we too got to go to the frantoio with the olives. One neighbor warned us solemnly that the frantoio owners generally tried to cheat the small grower and were not to be trusted. We earned our spurs in the first year by spotting a tiny error in the addition of the tallies much to the delight of our team and the discomfort of the frantoio storeman.

The first process

When the olives arrive at the frantoio, they are weighed in and put in the queue for processing. When our turn comes we unload the crates of olives into the pit of the washer and leaf remover. Leaves add an excessively bitter taste to the oil and are removed with a blower. From the washer the olives go through a rough milling process and are held there until the next part of the process is free.

The whole frantoio works on a continuous batch basis. "Continuous" in the sense that there is a flow of material through the whole complex from the receival pit to the spout for the oil, but "batch" in the sense that the olives of different owners go through in stages that are held at various points until the next stage is clear. There is no need to clear the whole complex from beginning to end before starting the next batch.

The frantoio we use has a capacity of about one tonne per hour but this tonne is made up of a series of separate batches from each grower. The batches weigh about 300 to 400 kg each. If you have more than this the fruit goes through in sequential batches and no attempt is made to keep them separate but if you have one batch (less than 300 kg will be processed) you are invited to inspect each step on the way to see that your olives have been moved to the next stage and are not contaminated by someone else's olives.

The crushing of the olives

From the rough mill the paste goes next to the actual operation of crushing. Our frantoio uses the traditional method of two huge granite wheels rotating in a basin. Strictly speaking this is the "frantoio" but the name has now been extended to the whole complex of machines. These wheels are over a metre in diameter and 30 cm wide and are driven round and round from a central shaft while the olive paste is continually pushed under the wheels by ploughs.

The wheel mill is a modern version of those used in Roman times and before. These were powered by a long shaft that stretched beyond the basin and were turned by a donkey or some other hapless animal. They still exist. We have seen them powered by camels in Tunisia.

Some of the modern plants use hammer mills instead of the stone wheels. From a quality point of view there seems to be little difference between the two methods. The hammer mill will produce a greener oil than the stone wheels but disperses the oil into an emulsion within the paste which means that in the next stage the paste has to be stirred for a longer time to coagulate the oil into drops that can be centrifuged out. Excessive stirring leads to oxidation of the oil.

Stirring the paste

This is an extremely important part of the process and it is here that all your efforts in the grove and in proper handling of the fruit can be destroyed. The two risky operations are the length of stirring and the degree of heating.

Experiments have shown that a decline in the polyphenol levels occurs during the stirring process. Stirring for too long reduces these vital polyphenols that are so important for flavor. If the stone wheels have been used there is no need to stir for more than half an hour at the most. If the process continues for two hours the stirred paste will have only a third or a quarter of those precious polyphenols left.

During the stirring operation the paste has to be heated to enable the oil to be extracted but the control of this heat is essential if the quality of the oil is not to be affected. The optimum temperature for quality oil is between 20° to 30° C. It is very difficult to extract oil when the process is operated at a temperature of less than 20°C. Many frantoio work at a higher temperature than 30°C because most growers want high extraction rates and a higher temperature achieves this. If the temperature is not much beyond 30°C the quality is not badly compromised, but it would be better if the optimum temperature was used. It may be possible to ask the frantoio owner to lower the temperature for a large batch and, if we really get into boutique oil, then we may try to do this.

We have seen olive oil in Australia labelled as "Cold pressed". When we asked what this signified, our frantoio owner said it was legal to call temperatures up to blood heat (37° C) "cold" but we are not sure whether this is true. If it is, 37°C is certainly higher than the optimum temperature for the production of a premium oil.

Separating the oil

Up to this stage, even though the machines are driven by electric motors, the basic process is very similar to that carried out a couple of thousands years ago. At the separating stage modernity reigns.

In the old days the paste from the grinding wheels would be put onto mats in the shape of car tyres which would then go onto a heavy hand operated press for the extraction.

The centrifuge press introduced a different system in which the paste flows through to an extractor which separates the paste into oil, water and solid, fairly dry residue (the sansa). This is called the three-phase method of processing. The early centrifuge machines produced poor quality oil because they required considerable amounts of water (often hot) added to the paste for extraction of the oil and because of this most of the polyphenols were lost.

Over the years the design improved and less water had to be added. The latest machines have what is called a two and half phase centrifuge. This separates the paste into oil, watery juice and sansa like the 3 phase machine but some of the watery juice extracted is recycled as a substitute for adding fresh water to the paste. This results in a better quality oil with less loss of polyphenols.

A 2 phase machine is also available which produces oil and very wet sansa. The quality of the oil is better than from the 3 phase machines and slightly better than the 2.5 phase machines but in Italy frantoio owners don't use these new machines much because they say that the sloppy slurry of sansa is impractical to store at the frantoio and they do not want the cost of carting it with all its extra water to the factory where it is processed for the residual oil.

Other extraction methods

Another system of extraction that is used here is commonly called the Rapanelli method after the manufacturer of the machines. Rapanelli is one of the famous three or four manufacturers of olive oil processing machinery based not far from us at Foligno. What impressed us most about their factory when we visited it was not all the gleaming new machines with fancy knobs and whiz bangs but some equipment they had built in 1934 for a frantoio in Turkey which had been sent back for reconditioning and which would go back there once the bearings and other worn parts had been replaced.

The oil in the Rapanelli machine is extracted from the paste by a gentle process of adhesion to paddles. It produces excellent quality oil with very high levels of flavor components but as it only extracts 50 to 60% of the potential oil the machine must be connected to a standard centrifuge to finish off the process. Naturally the capital cost is high.

Yet another method of extraction is Chiappini Press which is made by Nardi, one of the largest farm machinery manufacturers in Umbria. The Chiappini frantoio is at Fabro which is literally down the bottom of our hill. We have been told that the machine can be used for the extraction of other oils such as sunflowers. We have recently bought sesame oil milled from this press. Fabro is on the Chiana river and large quantities of sunflowers are grown along the river valley so the press is working for much longer periods in the year than the normal frantoio.

In spite of its proximity most of our information about it comes from Julian Archer's excellent book "***An introduction to olive oil processing.***"

During the course on olive harvesting and processing run by our local comune it was never mentioned so it cannot be widely used in Umbria. .

The final operation and "ecco il olio"

After the oil has been extracted it flows into a second centrifuge similar to an old fashioned milk separator to clean out the small amount of water left after it has passed through the main centrifuge. It is not a good idea to leave the oil and water in contact for too long. It will reduce the quality of the oil.

After this process the beautiful green oil flows into your drum. The suspended particles of the fruit thicken the green color. The big commercial people filter it to remove these but we love the oil just as it comes from the centrifuge. After a few weeks most of the sediment will have settled but the oil will remain a little cloudy. The sight and delicious smell of fresh oil is most satisfying. Most produce disappears into a factory and comes out much later as a bulk product but the oil produced from your own olive grove is poured out into your own drum right before your eyes. We can understand the resistance of the local farmers to suggestions that they bulk up their olives with their neighbors. It may be the logical way to improve quality but it takes away so much of the satisfaction.

When we have squeezed the last drop of oil out of the final centrifuge we weigh the oil so we can calculated the oil percentage and oil yield. These are all measured in kilos. Oil percentage is kilos of oil over kilos of fresh olives. Olive oil is lighter than water so a kilo of oil is more than a litre. If you are selling your oil you need to be clear about whether you are talking litres or kilos. The conversion of kilos to litres amounts to about 3 or 4% which is handy if you are bottling and selling it yourself as it gives you a little to play with after you have let the sediment settle.

Frantoio and costs

Our frantoio charges $AUS28 to process each quintale of fresh olives. All the farmers here use quintales - that is 100 kg - as their measure. The frantoio will also take oil as payment if the olives crush at more than 15% oil in which case they take 10% of the oil.

Like so much associated with the olive industry in Umbria the economics of the frantoio are deeply mysterious. The frantoio operates twenty four hours a day when there are enough olives. Given the small lots this will be the equivalent of a throughput of say 200 quintale a day. The harvest period lasts perhaps a month but the frantoio will not be not flat out day and night for all 30 days so 500 tonnes of olives (which is probably an average throughput) at $280 per tonne might be a reasonable estimate. This comes to a gross income of $140,000 from which comes the wages of two workers required on shifts plus considerable gas and electricity. Even if the profit were to be $100,000 clear it does not sound much of a return on $750,000 which is the cost of installing a medium sized frantoio. It certainly shows that a good throughput is needed to break even.

Frantoio are opening and closing all the time so there is a constant opportunity for farmers to change over. Our owner had to persuade his friends and contacts first to come to his frantoio, and then to stay - and he also needs to continue to find new clients. He takes his holidays in November to run the frantoio (with his father and his wife) and his job as district clerk provides him with an excellent means of contacting all the growers in the comune area.

In Australia and New Zealand the olive industry is still young and in many districts the 500 tonnes required for economic operation do not exist near at hand. Working a spanking new frantoio with small quantities while waiting for the 500 tonnes to materialise will be an expensive exercise. A potential frantoio owner (or a cooperative of growers who want to establish a frantoio) could consider using second-hand machinery.

In Italy there are some 12,000 frantoio which are constantly being modernised so there is a lot of second-hand and reconditioned equipment available at a fraction of the price of new. While the quality of the processing may not be as good as the most modern plant, it is much less costly than having a new plant working at a tiny fraction of its capacity for years. If the

Turks think that it is worth reconditioning their 1934 Rapanelli plant - even if it is only as a back up - it would certainly be worthwhile with newer equipment than this.

The mini frantoio

Mini frantoio are used by some growers who want to be self-sufficient. We cannot write from direct experience but we have a friend nearby who started full of enthusiasm to process his own oil but soon found it easier and cheaper to concentrate on the production and harvesting. He now takes all his olives to the local frantoio.

We have seen these mini frantoio in action only at the Bologna farm machinery fair and in Blenheim, NZ. They are made near Perugia, not far from here, and cost about $AUS 10,000. While the motors for the mill and press are hard wired there appears to be no other installation costs and a special building is not needed.

The mini frantoio is designed using the principles that governed the old presses that go back thousands of years but they incorporate modern materials.

The frantoio consists of three parts. The first is a hammer mill that smashes the olives into a paste. This is operated with a 3.5 HP electric motor so it should be well within the capacity of normal farm electricity supplies even those dependent on the single wire system.

The second is the press. The ancient method was to put the paste onto a woven mat in the shape of a tyre. A number of mats were then placed one above the other with a post through the middle and pressed with either a very long lever (usually a tree trunk) or a big screw. One finds these ancient presses in museums throughout Italy.

The modern mini-press uses the same principle but uses nylon woven mats and a hydraulic ram. Hydraulic pressure is provided with a pump and 1.3 HP electric motor so even with the hammer mill operating there should be no electric supply problems. It may be feasible to use a tractor PTO to run the hammer mill and the hydraulics to run the press if the electric supply is insufficient.

The final stage is simply a stainless steel tank of 140 litres capacity in which the liquid from the pressing goes. The oil comes to the top and the water settles to the bottom and they are separated by decanting off the oil.

This press could be described as a cold-cold pressing as the paste of smashed olives is the same temperature as the storage shed. Here in Italy that would probably be 5° C but it would probably be higher in Australia or

New Zealand. It is said that the decanting method of separation is not very efficient and that in the past heat was applied to improve separation thus reducing the quality of the oil. However the makers of this small mill from Perugia claim an excellent quality oil is produced and that the recovery rate is also good.

From our experience with wine presses of this type it is not possible to rush the pressing. One applies pressure, the juice oozes out, one applies more pressure and so on. It is not possible to hurry this up by applying more pressure in the expectation that all the juice will be extracted in a few minutes. In fact the manufacturers state that the cycle for each pressing is 50 minutes. Other books we have read on processing state that this might be too optimistic and pressing will take longer. The filling and emptying of the mats can take place while the other set are being pressed. The capacity of the whole frantoio could be increased by installing two presses. We have not checked with the manufacturers but it may be possible to fill the two presses from the same crusher and run them from the same hydraulic pump. If this were so the capacity of the whole plant could be doubled for a lot less than double the investment.

The plant does not have any olive cleaning or leaf removal section as found in the larger frantoio but this could easily be improvised. The old method of cleaning the leaves was to use a sieve or riddle made from wooden battens far enough apart to let the leaves through but not the olives. This was set up at an angle and the olives worked down the slope by hand. For small lots a similar device could be built and a more sophisticated version to shake the olives down the slope would not cost a great deal. The olives can easily be washed in a drum in batches if one is only pressing 50 to 100 kg per hour and more leaves can be removed during washing as they float to the top of the water bath.

The throughput of this type of frantoio is low. About 50/60 kg of olives can be pressed every hour. This should produce about 7 to 12 kg of oil. We are not sure whether the plant can be operated single handed but we would think so as otherwise the cost of processing would be very high indeed. It could be operated either at night just to handle the owner's own crop or on a shift basis day and night to process the crop of neighboring growers as well - although at a fee of $28 per 100 kg or $14 an hour this would not be very profitable. For a small producer this mini-frantoio could be a proposition if there is no other frantoio within reasonable travelling distance. We would travel quite some distance to avoid having one.

Chapter 8

THE MYSTERIES OF THE BOTTLE

Storing the oil to retain flavor

The Italian saying is *"Olio nuovo e vino vecchio"* - young oil and old wine. Most of our local farmers have a taste for the strong flavors of the fresh oil and start using the new oil on their bruschetta immediately. The stocks of last year's oil are put aside to be used for cooking. We were told by our neighbors to rack the new oil off the sediment in January - that is a couple of months after pressing. Good Italian restaurants in the country also feature the new oil on their tables about a month or two after harvest.

In the past the oil was stored in large terra cotta, Ali Baba jars of about 200 litres. These were glazed on the inside and acquired a black patina outside from the spilt oil. They had loose fitting wooden lids and stones were placed on top to keep rats and mice out. They love olive oil and will climb anything to get to it. The larger producers still use these jars as they are not only good storage vessels but provide a marvellous talking point for visitors to the storage cellars - part of "nostalgia marketing". They are still made in Italy but many of them are sold for ornamental purposes in gardens and are not glazed on the inside. These unglazed pots should not be used for oil storage. It is possible to buy the glazed ones and they are worth considering more from the marketing viewpoint than economical storage. There is a whole range of sizes down to about 15 litres. We have a 25 litre jar in our larder which we bought for about $50 from our local potter. We bought another 25 litre jar for $130 but it is really more like an amphora with two handles and is glazed on the outside as well as the inside. The really large ones of 200 litres cost $700 or $800.

For purely practical purposes everyone uses stainless steel or glass. A 50 litre stainless container with a tap costs about $80 and has a wide screw lid so the drum can be cleaned easily. If the oil is left in the drum for a year or more without racking (not a good idea) the sediment can be quite hard and difficult to remove if the container has a narrow neck. Smaller sizes are available in stainless steel but the price per litre rises steeply and most people use glass jars for 5 or 10 litre quantities. These jars also have a wide neck and are usually sold fitted in a plastic crate packed with straw.

For transport many growers use plastic Jerry cans made from special food grade plastic. They say it is fine for storage as well but we are not convinced. We are particularly sensitive to this as our neighbor used to deliver our share of oil in one of these plastic cans. A few minutes after it had been delivered on one occasion, we found that it had sprung a leak and only rapid emergency decanting saved us from finding all our new oil in a puddle on the floor the following day.

Long term storage can lead to the degradation of the oil particularly if there has been considerable contact with the air. The different "off" flavors are described as "heated", "old", and "rancid". The softer, "sweet" oils tend to spoil after some months, but the strong, bitter oil of Umbria can remain sound for up to two years.

Most of the larger oil producers mature the oil for some months. This lets the solids settle out and reduces the very strong bitter flavors. The commercial bottlers will probably filter the oil. There is now an increasing trend to sell some of the new oil under the label of "novello" within weeks of harvest and long before stocks of the previous harvest have run out. This is the usual gambit of turning the natural, farmer practise into a high-priced exoticism.

Labels and how to read them

If you have to either make your own labels or, worse, have to buy your oil from the boutique or supermarket, the mystery that surrounds labelling terms has to be pierced. Over the years, but particularly, since olive oil has become such a desirable commodity, much confusion has arisen over just what is meant by "extra vergine", cold pressed, hand picked and so on. You don't want to pay more for what is either an advertising fantasy or just normal practice.

We know of one producer here who sent his oil out into the wide world and got away with charging a rather hefty premium by labelling his bottles "hand picked" as though hand picking conferred some mysterious guarantee of top quality. The image of the concerned grower and his devoted helpers carefully picking the olives one by one (probably under a sunny sky) was powerful enough to make innocent consumers part with hard cash in the belief that they were purchasing some precious aspect of ancient country life. We old growers know that most oil comes from olives handpicked under cold grey skies and that, although it is a costly operation, it is not unique.

Anglo Saxon attitudes to labelling

A great deal of misunderstanding about the processes of oil production are encapsulated on labels and in articles about olive oil outside the

Mediterranean zone. And, to be honest, there are some pretty fantastic descriptions on labels written within the zone!

One such was a British magazine (described in the *Guardian* as being "admired worldwide for its high-quality editorial content" and in *Vogue* as "horticulture's style bible") which published a guide to "the sweetest-tasting olives and oils" and set about explaining the meaning behind labelling terms.

The author criticised labelling that emphasises acidity as a mark of quality as misleading and rightly pointed out that it neglects to make the distinction between untreated oil and chemically refined oil.

He went on to tell his readers that, in his opinion, *"hand-picked"* is the ultimate indicator of quality *"since olives ripen unevenly and each tree must be visited many times during the picking season."* Hand picking certainly is the way to get the best quality oil. After all most small growers hand pick their olives but they pick the whole crop at the one time gathering the fruit in various stages of maturity. They deliberately pick early because that is when the flavor is strong. The idea of visiting the tree many times to pick only the mature olives is ridiculous. To claim that mature olives make the best oil completely negates all practical and scientific knowledge on quality which decrees that early picked fruit has more flavor because some of it is green. The major criticism by growers of mechanical picking using shakers is that the fruit has to be mature for the shaker to work efficiently and this diminishes the flavor and tends to increase the acidity of the oil.

There are some groves in Liguria where nets are permanently set under the trees and the very mature olives fall into these nets to be gathered several times by growers. From our own observation of this area this method of harvesting has more to do with the extremely steep mountain sides on which the trees are growing and the danger that would be encountered if nets were moved from tree to tree and the pickers had to climb very unstable ladders than with any desire to improve the quality of the oil.

The terms *"cold press"* and *"first pressing"* were described in the article as *"clues to quality oil"*. They may be clues but they are not a guarantee and are open to differing interpretations. The labels extravergine, vergine or olive oil are all "first pressed" oil yet the quality of each is different and so is the flavor. It is possible to label oil of poor quality and little flavor as "cold" or "first pressed". These days, with modern machinery, the only oil that is second pressed is oil of sansa which is extracted from paste residues by heat and solvents.

"Cold-pressed" is a difficult term to define. Cold in reference to what? Ambient temperature? Our first lot of olives went into the frantoio this year at only a few degrees above freezing but in Tunisia they may be 15°C or more when they are pressed. The reality is that the olive paste is nearly always heated at the frantoio and there is little reduction in quality provided the temperature is no more than 30° C. And the regulations say that oil heated to 37°C can be labelled "cold-pressed".

There is a further quibble when the author says that "*Single estate extra virgin oil is often a single variety from an olive estate, and purer than a commercially-blended extra virgin oil which, like a vin de table from a co-operative, is blended to a consistent style.*"

It is correct to say that commercially blended oil is often like a "vin de table" and is a blend of various quality oils from various destinations, but rarely does an estate bottle oil come from only one variety of tree. The norm is to bottle oil pressed from the mix of varieties on the estate. There is always a mixture because of the need to achieve good cross pollination. The unique quality comes not just from the varieties grown there, but from the altitude, the soil type, the climate of the region and the management of the grower.

Some years ago we explained to an Italian friend that Queenslanders were called "banana benders" because bananas grow naturally straight and have to be bent by hand. They believed us for a full ten seconds which we thought a triumph. There must be a triumphant Italian laughing somewhere in the knowledge that his olive picking story was not only believed for more than ten seconds but has also appeared in print in the British "horticultural bible".

Classification for labelling

The complexity that hits the general consumer in the eye comes when they have to interpret the classifications put on commercial oil labelling by various regulating bodies.

The classification of olive oil is determined by European Union law and as most of the world production takes place in the European Union these grades are effectively the international standards for olive oil. In 1992 the law was simplified from the seven grades of oil that had applied since 1960 to four for retail purposes.

When oil that does not fit these standards is sold on to processors for blending, other definitions are used to describe the oil.

The four classifications that appear on bottles in shops are:

Olio extravergine di oliva - (English: Extra virgin olive oil)
This does not mean that the oil is pressed by virgins. It simply means that

it is pure olive oil. It has had no other vegetable oil blended with it but it can be a blend of various olive oils. The oil has had no chemical treatment, and has an acid content of less than 1 gm per 100 gm (1%) measured in oleic acid. The acidity of the oil is a measure of its rancidity. The higher the level of acid in the oil the more likely it is to be rancid.

Some of the better known brands in Italy were tested by a consumer magazine called *Altroconsumo* in 1990. These tests showed that the actual acidity of a selection of oils from the supermarket varied from as low as 0.3% to 0.9%.

Olio vergine di oliva - (English: Virgin olive oil)

The acidity and rancidity is of this oil is higher but it is still a pure olive oil and has not been chemically treated. To conform to this label the acidity level can be up to 2 gm/100 gm (2%). While this grade exists in law in fact it is very rarely seen in Italian supermarkets. Perhaps the bottlers blend it with very low acidity oil to enlarge their supplies of oil that meet the extravergine standard - we don't know.

Olio di oliva - (English: Olive oil)

While the maximum acidity of this oil has to be no more than 1.5 gm/ 100 gm when bottled, the oil has been treated or refined to reduce its original acidity by chemical processing with caustic soda. In *Altroconsumo's* tests the acidity of this oil in the bottle was generally lower than the extravergine - from 0.1% to 0.4% with only one oil of 0.9%.

Olio di sansa e di oliva

This is a blend of chemically treated olive oil and some oil extracted with heat and solvents from the sansa - that is the cake residue left from the frantoio. The oil from the sansa has a high acidity level and has been treated chemically to reduce it. The maximum acidity for this grade of oil is 1.5 gm/ 100 gm (1.5%).

Other labelling

Here we get into a field that is both confusing and ambiguous. To the uninitiated it can be misleading. In Australia and New Zealand and generally outside the main olive oil producing countries, we see labels like these:

Olive oil or Pure olive oil

This is the most common grade of oil sold in Australia and New Zealand

and is the same as "Olio di oliva". The oil has been refined with chemicals to reduce the acidity. "Olive oil" is an accurate description of the content but the addition of the word "pure" seems inappropriate. Once oil has been treated with chemicals it may be only a little unpure, but it is no longer the natural product.

Extra Light

This is the same as "olive oil" or "olio di oliva" above. That is it has been chemically treated to reduce the original acidity. The "extra light" refers to the lack of flavor and color. This usually means that the oil is from varieties that do not have a great deal of flavor and of course the chemical treatment reduces this even further. Elsewhere in the food industry "light" has been used to imply that the product has fewer calories per unit of product and this is usually achieved by the addition of more water and emulsifying agents or detergents. This is not the case with "extra light" olive oil. It has not been emulsified with water and has the same calories as the other olive oils.

First pressing

Another description that sometimes appears on labels is "First pressing". In fact nearly all olive oil is first pressing. The only exception is a the olio di sansa - which results from a second pressing of the olive paste using heat and solvents. This is labelled as "olio di sansa".

Cold pressed

According to the International Olive Oil Council in Madrid this indicates that the oil has been pressed at less than 37°C. This is in reality an excessive temperature for pressing (the optimum is between 20 to 30°C) so there is some doubt as to whether it means anything at all. It seems to be a rather doubtful attempt to increase the price, rather than to inform the consumer in a helpful way.

The danger to the industry is that these misleading labels can create the same mistrust for olive oil that consumers developed when marketing groups played games with packs of orange juice.

What does good taste mean?

Grades of olive oil based on acidity are "commodity" descriptions based on chemical analysis. Premium oils have flavor, color and nose that go beyond the extravergine classification. We doubt whether anyone but a trained expert would be able to pick the differences in acidity by taste alone. We tasted an extravergine oil in New Zealand made from *Barnea* olives which claimed one of the lowest acidity levels ever tested. The taste was so bland that one might as well have bought a cheap extravergine from the local supermarket.

In the old days wine was graded on its alcohol content. A good level of alcohol was important to ensure that the wine kept well. With modern techniques even low alcohol wine can be kept safely and we use the characteristics such as flavor and nose to distinguish good wines from the mediocre. Extravergine oils are the same - they can vary from excellent (premium) oils to also-ran. In saying this, we do not mean to imply that the classifications of olive oil by acidity are useless and can be ignored. Acidity is important for the keeping qualities of the oil but the terms used to describe premium oils are in some ways similar to those used for wine.

Nose

Oil is described as *"fruity"* when it has a pronounced nose. The smell of the fresh fruit comes through to the oil. When the oil comes from olives that have been picked late, the nose is described as *"mature fruity"* . When the oil comes from olives that have been picked from partly green fruit the nose is described as *"green fruity"*. Some people prefer one, others prefer the other. It is in fact a matter of personal taste.

Nose is due to volatile constituents:-

* Aliphatic alcohols.
* Diterpenic alcohols.
* Triterpenic alcohols.
* Unsaturated alcohols.
* Saturated and unsaturated aldehydes.
* Ketones.
* Esters.

Nose depends on:-

* Variety.
* Ripening stage particularly fruit color.
* Condition of fruit at pressing.
* Method of oil extraction.
* Storage period and method of storage.
* Further refining of oil

Flavor

"Sweet" - this is not meant literally as olive oil has no sugar but is used as an opposite to bitter. In Umbria the sweet or *dolce* oils are sneered at but in other parts of Italy such as Liguria and in other Mediterranean countries they

are highly regarded - it all depends on personal taste, just as some people prefer sweet wine and some dry there are some who prefer sweet oil and some bitter.

"Bitter" - this is the bitter taste of the fresh olive coming through to the oil. We have become hooked on the strong, bitter oils that are characteristic of our region. It is characteristic of oils that have been produced from olives that are partly green. These in turn come from the cooler marginal areas where olives mature in the autumn without becoming fully pigmented.

"Spicy" - this taste can be separated out from the bitter and is also stronger in oils obtained from partly green olives.

"Grassy ", *"almond"* and *"apple"* are also used at times to describe particular flavors.

Flavor is due to:

  * Fatty acids
  * Polyphenols.

Flavor depends on:-

  * Variety
  * Ripening stage particularly color of fruit
  * Condition of fruit at pressing
  * Storage period and method
  * Further refining of the oil.

Color

The color of the oil can be golden or green. There seems to be some conflict among experts about the importance of color with the Tuscans in general saying the green color is not important for the flavor of the oil while in Umbria we produce more green oils and say it is important.

From our own experience the green color always produces gasps of appreciation from our visitors. Whether they would pick up any flavor differences if they were blind-folded may be doubtful but as they are not eating blind-folded the green color becomes part of the pleasure of appreciating a premium oil.

Color is due to Lipo-soluble (fat soluble) pigments:-

  * Chlorophyll (green)
  * Xanthophylls (yellow)
  * Carotenes (yellow -red).

Color depends on:

  * Variety

* Ripening stage particularly the color of the fruit at harvest
* The condition or freshness of the fruit when pressed.

More on taste

This is obviously the most important quality characteristic for premium oils. Like all tastes it is difficult to measure chemically and the human taste buds are much more precise than chemical analysis. Having said this there seems to be a strong relationship between the taste of premium oils and the level of polyphenols. To give some idea of the way in which polyphenol measurement can denote taste here are some tasting comments related to the polyphenol content of some Tuscan oils tested by the Giunta di Toscana.

Taste characteristic:	Polyphenol content in mg/kg of olive oil
Sweet, apple, wood	137
Pungent, light fruit and bitter leaf flavor	219
Very pungent, fruity, slightly bitter leaf flavor	240
Very pungent, fruity, slightly bitter leaf flavor	260
Bitter and pungent	336
Leaf flavor	450
Strongly pungent, bitter, anomalous flavor	616
Unpleasant, strong leaf flavor	706
Unpleasant, strong leaf flavor	826
Unpleasant, strong leaf flavor	992

It seems that the optimum level of polyphenols for pleasant taste is between about 200 and 350 mg/Kg of oil. Oils with less than these levels are insipid and those above this level have an unpleasantly strong and leafy taste. The higher levels of polyphenols will ensure that the oils will keep well - they will also be good in the second year - and the strong bitter taste will soften. These very strongly flavored oils may be usefully blended with bland oils to improve the overall quality and flavor.

Varietal influence on taste

The following is a comparison made by the Giunta di Toscana of some common Tuscan olive varieties showing the relative levels of polyphenols. The amount of polyphenols is not fixed any more than the oil percentage is fixed but will vary in different climatic conditions.

Variety	Harvest date	Acidity gm/100 gm	Total polyphenols mg/Kg
Frantoio	6.12.83	0.29	346
	13.12.83	0.28	431
Moraiolo	6.12.83	0.31	589
	13.12.83	0.26	536
Maurino	13.12.83	0.90	444

One must be careful with the interpretation of these figures. They are comparisons only and although they show that *Moraiolo* has a polyphenol level that is 30 to 50% higher than *Frantoio*, the actual level will depend on seasonal conditions and the picking time.

The brand on the label

At present there are two systems of labelling in operation in Italy. There is the "brand name" system and the "grower" system. A good example of the brand name system is the Australian wine industry where less than half a dozen big companies dominate more than 85% of the market. They promote their brands and sub brands on domestic and export markets with very little reference to where the grapes were grown. A common description on an export label is "south eastern Australia" which covers the whole of South Australia, Victoria and Tasmania. The wine industry has demonstrated the success of the system. These wines provide excellent value for money and for many consumers reliability of the brand and sub brand is sufficient.

Most olive oil sold inside and outside Italy is labelled in this manner. A few large brands dominate the market and some attract very high prices because they have acquired a particular status. The whole purpose of "brand" marketing is to build up an image in the consumers' mind and avoid comparisons with other oils. They want the brand to be isolated from the others so price and quality comparisons on the part of the consumer are more difficult. The brand becomes the selling focus rather than the content of the bottle.

The grower label

At the other end of the scale is the "grower" system which can be seen in operation in the French wine industry as "appellation controlée" or "truth in labelling" where the "truth" applies primarily to the place the product was grown. There is a similar system in Italy called DOC or DOCG which applies to wine, olive oil and many other products.

The grower system of labelling is more important in Europe. It hardly exists in the Anglo - Saxon world. The grower system is fiercely criticised by the owners of important brands such as the Australian wine companies as they claim it stifles innovation and is full of bureaucratic rules that have little to do with quality.

It is true that the most famous grower schemes such as Champagne, Burgundy and Bordeaux have set in concrete many local rules that are unimportant for quality, but, as long as they consistently manage to produce the highest priced wines in the world, the growers are unlikely to change this winning formula. The Chianti scheme in Tuscany has got itself into a muddle by controlling the percentage of the grape variety *Sangiovese* in Chianti DOC to such an extent that the best "Super Tuscan" wines are effectively given the lowest wine classification because they contain more *Cabernet Sauvignon* and less *Sangiovese* than is allowed. Other newer grower schemes such as that in the wine growing district of Cahors in south west France demonstrate that the grower system can be adaptable and free from pointless control. They have resuscitated an *Appellation Controlée* district that had fallen into dissolution due to disease and is now considered one of the best districts for red wine in France.

The real, but unstated, opposition to the grower schemes is that they are based on a territory. Marketing power is with the owner of the land not the owners of the brand.

We do not think the grower schemes are perfect. The most legitimate criticism is that they are, like the brand schemes, arrogant in their attitude to the consumer. They produce a set of rules, the most important of which are the territorial limits of the district name and the varieties that can be used, but they pass very little of this information on to the consumer. The attitude is - we are the experts, trust us and have faith in the "name" of our district. It is very similar to "trust our brand".

In Italy with olive oil the situation is made worse by the fact that the DOC or DOCG districts are almost impossible to identify if you live outside the country and hard to locate if you live in another region. Italian addresses are difficult to follow, even for Italians. Often the DOC is simply a collection of little known villages and the address is further obscured because the DOC districts are based on provinces not regions which are only identified by initials. Even when the initials divulge the region, Perugia is reasonably well known but who has heard of Terni outside Italy. Yet they are the two large and important provinces of Umbria.

Consumer-friendly labels

Obviously with the big brand names it would be better if misleading labels such as "pure" for third grade olive oil and "extra light" for low flavored oil were not used. It would also be better if the country of origin was stated but these oils are blends and there is not much more that can be said.

For the premium oils that are produced under the DOC or DOCG schemes there should be much more information. Firstly the district should be clearly identified on a map for the uninitiated. They should also be independently classified into high, medium and low altitude or cool climate or some such description that will indicate to the consumer the style of oil that might be expected. The date the oil was crushed should be stated.

The varieties used should be stated - not necessarily every one but a general description such as "at least 50% *Moraiolo* and 25% *Frantoio*". At present varieties may not mean much to the average consumer but wine varieties did not mean much either a few decades ago yet they now trip off the tongue of every wine buff. Obviously such terms as "cold pressed" and "first pressing" should be avoided but the actual temperature would be useful additional information.

Future labelling rules

The rules governing the labelling of olive oil are in a mess. The Italians admit it and are drafting new rules but the process of consultation is protracted and they are not expected to be in force for some years. Whether they will provide consumers with significantly more information is an open question given the power of the big bottlers and blenders. Certainly the consumer cooperatives (who run supermarkets here) are strong in Italy and have traditionally supported the Left parties that form the present government so there may be a glimmer of hope ahead.

Chapter 9

THE MARKET FOR OLIVE OIL

The miracle of the disappearing olive oil

Italy and Spain are by far the two largest producers in the world. It may seem strange but Italy is the largest importer of oil - about 300,000 tonnes annually and also the second largest exporter - about 150,000 tonnes. Spain is the largest exporter - about 300,000 tonnes annually. French farming friends we stayed with in the Cognac area used to refer jokingly to their tiny village of Clam as the centre of the world. We are only half joking when we refer to Umbria as the centre of the world of olive oil. Italy is the central country of the Mediterranean zone where 95% of the world's olive oil is produced and Umbria is roughly in the centre of Italy. It has to be admitted though that Tuscany is the important player in the trade, not Umbria.

St Francis gave Umbria its title of "land of saints" but the Tuscans perform the miracle of the olive oil every day. The 300,000 tonnes of imported oil is simply made to disappear. We have never seen a bottle of oil in Italy or Italian oil in Australia or NZ that has been labelled "Blend of Italian and Tunisian or Spanish or other oil" yet that must be the case. Tuscany exports more oil than it produces. The major olive oil blenders, bottlers and exporters are concentrated around Lucca in the north and they buy oil from other parts of Italy and other countries in the Mediterranean and sell it as their own both for local consumption and for export. To be fair they do not actually mislead by labelling it as "Produce of Italy" but they obviously hope that their Italian name and Tuscan address will give the impression that the oil is not only Italian but also Tuscan.

Trade in oil in the Mediterranean Basin

For thousands of years olive oil has been produced and consumed in the Mediterranean region. Olive oil has always been the basic cooking oil in North Africa, the Middle East, Greece, southern Italy and Spain. Country people picked and pressed their own oil and commercial supplies were cheap in cities and towns because labor costs were low.

After the Second World war the relative price of olive oil to the producer dropped. Plant breeding improved the yield of many other vegetable oils such as sunflower and canola (oilseed rape). When combined with mechanised harvesting they could be produced much more cheaply than olive oil. They became strong competitors in the basic cooking oil market in the Mediterranean .

Olive oil could not compete because picking was labor intensive and mechanical pickers had not been invented or developed. We have described the enormous shift of population from the Italian countryside to the cities, to Australia and to other countries that took place in the 1950's and 1960's. Spain and Greece experienced their rural depopulation some years later. Industrial wages attracted workers away from the country. There was no longer a plentiful supply of small farmers and destitute workers available to pick the olives.

Even though olive producers received subsidies under the Common Agricultural Policy of the European Union it was still a difficult period and many hundreds of thousands of trees were pulled out in Spain and other Mediterranean countries. International development organisations such as the World Bank and the World Food Program added to the marketing problems for olive oil by encouraging olive planting in the countries of North Africa and Turkey.

While conspiracy theories abound about the "secret agenda" of these international organisations, one has to wonder at the sanity of making large loans available to Ghana to plant coffee so they can diversify out of cocoa while, at the same time, making equally large loans to Uganda to pull out its coffee so it can diversify into cocoa. The olive oil story is very similar. Institutions lent money to farmers to plant olives when other enterprises such as sheep meat from improved legume pastures had so much greater potential return. Was this a conspiracy to help American and European meat exporters or plain stupidity?

It is said that the major reason for the lack of interest in olive oil production in the USA was due to the difficulty they had in competing with low priced oil from the Mediterranean. They turned to the production of preserved olives for eating and dry Martini popping instead.

World trade in olive oil

During the 19th century world trade in agricultural commodities expanded greatly with Britain, the world's wealthiest country at the time, being the centre. Australia and New Zealand were early partners in this trade which included not only basic food stuffs such as wheat, butter and meat but also wine, tea and coffee.

The British had imported wine in great quantities for many centuries. The development of port, sherry and cognac were all in response to the demand from the British market. In the nineteenth century, Bordeaux in France and Chianti in Italy were experiencing export booms for red wine that went to Britain. It was comparatively easy for the Australian wine producers to fit into this established wine market and they did very well out of it. There was no British market or any world trade for olives or olive oil with the exception of very low grade oil for soap manufacture. The only Mediterranean trade came from Italy which was exporting oil from Naples to France for soap making in the 19th century long before Palmolive had been thought of.

Anglo-Saxon attitudes to olive oil

Creating a market in Anglo-Saxon countries for olive oil was not easy. British tourists travelled to Italy and other Mediterranean countries for centuries to see the antiquities but they universally despised the food as being too "oily" and "stinking" of garlic. Eating it was the high price they had to pay for being cultured. Animal fats were the basis of British cooking and children were fed on bread and dripping and suet pudding. The wealthy had plenty of butter. Similar eating habits occurred throughout northern Europe and in America except where colonies of Italian and other Mediterranean immigrants had established themselves.

The British and Irish immigrants to Australia carried their food prejudices with them. An old established chemist in Adelaide bottled "Fauldings Olive Oil" which may have come from local production but was labelled "For medicinal use". No one considered that olive oil would be used from choice. We had a neighbor in the Barossa Valley who practised as a naturopath. His favorite medicine was large doses of olive oil which was considered to be nasty enough by his Anglo-Celtic patients to be an excellent cure.

I can remember when growing up in Adelaide in the 1950's the difficulties my mother had in purchasing vegetable oil of any type. To buy her vegetable oil (mostly peanut at that time) she had to go to a "continental" grocer in the city. "Continental" was a quaint British term for Europe which was transferred direct to Australia without any apparent conception of its strangeness in the continent of Australia. It is hard to believe with the universal availability of such things as vegetable oil and yoghourt in supermarkets in Australia and New Zealand today that only forty years ago they could only be purchased at exotic "continental" grocers and delis.

These British food preferences continued past the middle of the 20th century. It is still remembered in our village the day the British troops of the Eighth Army arrived to liberate the citizens from the Germans. The villagers' offered the soldiers their most precious product - olive oil - considered some of the best in Italy. The soldiers were grateful but puzzled. Their captain came to the padrone and, highly embarrassed, explained that the soldiers were unused to olive oil, but would be delighted to have some local wine. The exchange took place to mutual delight. The villagers still recount this story as an example of the bizarre food preferences of the British.

The transformation of eating habits

Since the early 1970s there has been a transformation of eating habits in Britain and other Anglo Saxon cultures and in other northern European countries. Vegetable oils have taken over half the market in countries such as Germany, Denmark and Britain which were the previously bastions of animal fats such as butter, lard, dripping and suet. Many northern European countries are now importing significant quantities of olive oil. While these imports are only a small proportion of the overall vegetable oil market the quantity of olive oil being imported is expanding rapidly. Similar changes have occurred in the USA

In Southern Europe, olive oil remains king, but other vegetable oils such as canola and sunflower have established a place in the kitchen (mainly for deep frying) which they have no difficulty in retaining.

Olive oil in the vegetable oil market

Fortunately the prospects for olive oil have improved considerably over the last several decades. Olive oil has now established its own market quite separate from other vegetable oils. The price of the olive oil at the bottom end of the market is still sensitive to the prices of other vegetable oils in the same way as the cheaper cask or box wines are sensitive to the prices for other alcoholic beverages. Quality olive oil has moved well clear of cooking oil prices and has become a condiment. It is similar to bottled wine which has cut itself completely free of the price of the cask. In our local Coop supermarket vegetable oils such as sunflower and canola sell at below $AUS3 a litre, the cheapest olive oil made by heat extraction of oil from the pressings of the frantoio (the sansa) is around $4 , and the cheapest "real" olive oil (but processed to reduce acidity) is $5. This is double the price of most vegetable oils.

Retail prices for quality olive oil

In Italy, oils labelled "extravergine" can be bought in the supermarket for as little as $8 a litre, although large containers of 5 litres on "special" are sometimes less than this. Prices go to about $18 a litre which is the limit that our supermarket thinks its customers will pay. The shelves are groaning with olive oils so people must be buying them in spite of the fact that they are more expensive than other oils.

Away from the supermarket, quality oils sell for well over $18 a litre. We did some research in the specialty shops of Perugia and found a number of excellent single grove oils that generally ranged in price from $25 to $35 a litre. The most expensive of all was one with individually numbered bottles for $52 a litre. Italian friends "in the trade" are sceptical about the value of oils above $35 a litre and consider that the high price is due to fancy publicity rather than real merit. This trawl through the olive oils in the supermarket and specialty shops confirms the enormous range in quality covered by the term "extravergine". In Italy consumers are well aware of quality and, with the possible exception of the $52 a litre oil, are able to judge precisely how much value they will get for their money.

Outside Italy the market seems to be dominated by the poorer grades of oil. Australia is a good example. In 1996 the average wholesale price of olive oil imported was $5.50 per litre. Extravergine oil which cost more accounted for an estimated 15 to 20% of imports so the average price of the remaining 80 to 85% must have been below $5 a litre.

Today there are tiny quantities of boutique oils being produced and sold in Australia and NZ. These are some of the most expensive in the world with retail prices ranging from $40 to 70 a litre.

Prices to the grower for olive oil

No doubt many prospective growers in Australia and New Zealand aim to supply this boutique market and receive a high price for their oil. The market is limited and it is questionable whether these high prices can be maintained once local production expands. Growers also need to be aware that the boutique producers are usually associated with a strong brand image. It may be one they have developed themselves from their status as pioneers in the industry or it may carry over from their winery or role as a celebrity chef. Growers in central Italy where the olive oil industry is well established receive $10 to $15 a litre for their premium extravergine oil.

At the bulk end of the market things are fairly desperate. Growers in

Tunisia who supply this market receive about $3 a litre and a rough calculation from the available statistics shows that growers in Australia and NZ should not expect much more for bulk oil. The Australian Bureau of Statistic figures we quoted above show that the price of imported bulk oil is less than $5 a litre. However the price for this oil includes the cost to the wholesaler of bulking, blending, branding, and bottling. Growers selling their oil directly to the wholesaler would therefore get an even lower price than $5 a litre. From their return they would have to pay the costs associated with the crushing of the olives. Currently this is between $1-2 per litre.

The effect of rising incomes in the producing countries

In spite of all the markets that are expanding so rapidly outside the Mediterranean zone (Ireland for example increased olive oil consumption by 9 times in the last ten years) olive oil is still overwhelmingly consumed in the countries that produce it.

The greatly improved standard of living in the two major producing countries, Italy and Spain, means that consumers are able to choose the oil they prefer rather than the oil they can afford. Ten years ago Italy celebrated the "overtaking" when annual income per head overtook that of Britain. While the devaluation of the Italian lire and the rise of the British pound has lowered the relative position of Italy since then the standard of living remains the same. Spain is still a long way behind both Britain and Italy in terms of standard of living but it has improved by an enormous amount over the last couple of decades. More people are now able to pay the higher price that olive oil commands.

This increased income in the Mediterranean region has also encouraged a shift towards the consumption of more good quality oil.

The health angle

The great explosion in olive oil consumption outside the Mediterranean region really got a boost when advertisers tied olive oil to good health. Given that the taste of oil is only beginning to be appreciated, this may well have started the boom.

The health advantage of olive oil is primarily due to the favorable balance between mono-unsaturated and poly-unsaturated fatty acids and the moderate amount of saturated fatty acids in it.

Olive oil is a mixture of unsaturated and saturated fats. According to the International Olive Oil Council the composition of olive oil is:

Mono - unsaturated Oleic .... 70 - 80%
Poly - unsaturated Linoleic .... 6 - 9%
Saturated Palmitic .... 8 - 15%
Saturated Stearic .... 1.5 - 3%

There is some difference between varieties with *Frantoio* having a high ratio of unsaturated fat to saturated of 5.66 and *Maurino* having a comparatively low ratio of 4.98.

The high content of oleic (mono-unsaturated) fat in olive oil varies considerably more than the average figures given by the International Olive Oil Council. For example, oil produced in Tunisia, where olives ripen in the hot, late summer has as little as 56% oleic content while oil produced in the much cooler high country of central Italy has as much as 84%. It may be that those consumers who use olive oil specifically for their health will eventually seek out cool climate oils to ensure a higher content of oleic.

As well as the unsaturated fatty acids in olive oil there are other health benefits. The polyphenols are anti-oxidants and are important in breaking down cholesterol. They are present in olive oil in much larger quantities than in other vegetable oils but there is considerable variation and the cool regions again score the highest marks for content. In addition, the pigments such as chlorophyll and carotene which are present in olive oil contain substances which it is claimed prevent the absorption of cholesterol in the intestine.

Low grade oil becomes less of a health food when it is refined by the addition of alkalines to reduce the acidity or extracted from sansa. These processes either drastically reduce or destroy the vitamins and anti-oxidants. It is ironic that the markets that seem to have taken to olive oil for its health properties such as the USA and Australia import large quantities of low grade oil in which the health giving components are at their lowest level. If consumers think that "extra light" is somehow an even healthier grade of oil they will be disappointed as it is on the low end of the scale for health ingredients.

More worrying is the use of the image of healthy olive oil to sell "spreads" containing small quantities of olive oil. An example is Olivio Spread, now being sold in Britain but coming to your supermarket soon. It is advertised as providing the health properties of the Mediterranean diet. To be fair it is labelled as "with" olive oil which allows the manufacturer to mix in other vegetable oils without actually lying. The processing will have destroyed the vitamins and anti-oxidants as well as introducing a range of emulsifiers that are needed to keep the high water content stable.

This adulteration of natural, healthy food is widespread. Processors frequently use the image of the original to sell it but adulterate the natural product in a manner that deprives the consumer of the very benefits that make the original product attractive.

Many farmers have suffered from loss of markets due to the bad name their product generates among consumers after processors have had their way with it.

Scientific research

As far as we know no one has even attempted to measure the finer details of the health benefits of premium olive oil versus other olive oils.

Scientific research seems to indicate there are differences. It could be argued that all olive oil is comparatively healthy and one should not worry about the finer points of polyphenols or the unsaturated fat ratio of particular varieties. This type of research adds integrity to the claims of those who promote the health aspect of oil. If we truly believe they are important this will increase our insistence on them being there. If we brush them aside we run the risk of allowing flavor/health becoming a subsidiary aspect of oil in the same way as has happened with tomatoes and many other "genetically improved" fruits and vegetables.

Many nutritionalists promote the "Mediterranean diet" as a more healthy way of eating. The scientific basis for this promotion is the work of Professor Keys who made a comparison of diets in seven countries - USA, Yugoslavia, Finland, Japan, South Africa, Italy and Greece. He identified Greece and southern Italy as having the best diet from the point of view of health.

The diet includes more fruit, more salads, and more grains than in most Western diets, and, of course, more olive oil. Prof. Keys considers the consumption of olive oil to be a major factor in the better health of Greeks and Italians. The greatest contrast was between Finland where the diet includes a very high proportion of animals fats and Greece where olive oil is used. The death rate from cardiovascular disease is five times higher in Finland than in Greece.

An Italian study conducted on the same lines showed that the death rate from cardiovascular disease varied from 111 per 100,000 people in the Val d' Aosta near the Swiss border where a high proportion of animal fats are eaten, to 38 per 100,000 in Sicily where olive oil and other vegetable oils are universally used.

It is of course extremely difficult to draw firm conclusions from this type of survey data and there have been other studies that have shown that death rates are very low in parts of France where local diets include large quantities of animal fat. We suspect that the high intake of fruit, grain and vegetables may also be quite important in accounting for the good health of those who eat in Mediterranean countries.

The Mediterranean diet has now achieved world wide fame, not just in the USA where Professor Keys works, but in many other countries where the consumption of high levels of animal fats are a tradition. The European Union is now actively promoting the Mediterranean diet. The result is an increase in the consumption of olive oil in countries outside the Mediterranean region.

Other healthy oils

The emphasis on the health properties of olive oil particularly outside the Mediterranean has certainly proved a powerful marketing tool but one needs to be cautious about constructing a whole industry on a single concept. Olive oil is not the only oil to be promoted for its health properties. Other studies have shown that some Japanese and Eskimo fishing communities have very low rates of heart disease. It has been found that the important factor in their diet is fish oils that contain a particular unsaturated fat called DHA.

The same type of unsaturated fat occurs in a number of vegetable seed oils such a canola and Indian mustard. Indian mustard is a particularly rich source. Mustard oil is an important component of Indian food and has the same condiment value as olive oil in Italian food. Presently Western plant breeders, interested in the health giving properties of mustard oil, are attempting to remove the strong flavor from the oil, blissfully unaware that without the flavor, the oil loses its character.

These particular oils are potential competitors with olive oil as the source of healthy living.

The nostalgia market

Before the Second World War, Tate and Lyle sold their sugar in Britain with the slogan "Untouched by human hand". It was the period when science and technology represented hygiene, modernity and purity. Since then science and technology have fouled their own nest and consumers are now more likely to respond to "Untouched by machine and chemical free". Olive oil has a great advantage for this type of demand.

The nostalgia for the past when food was free from chemical contamination can be realised with olive oil. Olive oil production has been less influenced by the scientific and technological revolution than most agricultural crops. We have already mentioned the fact that most of the olives in this zone are not sprayed with fungicides or insecticides and only a few growers use chemical fertilisers. Most of the picking is still done by hand. Farmers who grow cereals and many other field crops have had to change their farming systems in a quite radical manner in order to meet labelling requirements if they wish to sell their product as "organic" and gain the premium that such a label is attracting. Many growers are already growing "organic" olives but somewhat surprisingly they do not yet appear to widely exploit this as a marketing tool.

The major difference between olive oil production now and one thousand years ago is in the processing and in spite of all attempts by food writers to create a nostalgic aura around the old presses the modern equipment is excellent if used correctly and the standard of the oil has improved greatly since it was introduced.

But nostalgia does sell product and new countries entering the field will no doubt rapidly construct a mystique consisting of Italian or Greek grandparents, pioneer trees, and sheds under gum trees where hand picked olives are hand pressed, hand bottled, and hand labelled before being handed over to the supermarket and the glad hand of the consumer. The word "hand" attached to any product works magic in transforming it to a highly desirable product with overtones of "once upon a time". I once remember a "wannabee" cousin telling me in awed tones that her wedding cake was "hand iced". Have you ever tried to ice a wedding cake with a machine?

Chapter 10

OLIVE OIL IN FOOD AND OTHER USES

Olive oil in food

Italian food is the fastest growing "fashionable" cuisine in the world. The insulting epithets of "oily" and "stinking of garlic" are no longer used by food writers and travellers. Now they drool over olive oil and make bruschetta reeking of garlic. Italian restaurants and take-aways have spread throughout the world and dishes such as pizza, spaghetti and ravioli are eaten in vast quantities in countries that despised them less than fifty years ago. The latest bread craze is focaccia which has oil in the dough and is brushed with olive oil before baking. The passion for "Italian" is not confined to eating out but has been absorbed into the diet eaten at home.

A great part of the Italian cuisine that has taken the world by storm comes from the south and centre of Italy - the areas that use olive oil daily. In the north of Italy butter, cream and other animal fats are frequently used. While cheaper vegetable oils are often used in the preparation of take-away and frozen food there is a growing appreciation among consumers worldwide that olive oil is essential for genuine Italian food.

A typical Italian meal

Italian restaurants succeed only if they produce food as near as possible to the food Italians eat in their own homes. The desire for recherché and sometimes bizarre ingredients now so common in Anglo Saxon restaurants is not admired here. Italian chefs who try to pursue this path are rapidly left with no clients until they change their menus back to traditional Italian dishes.

Italians may travel the world on business, but they are not happy in countries where they cannot find good Italian food.

This affects the Chinese and other ethnic restaurants that try to cater in Italy for those who want something different. It's never long before the menus are heavily infiltrated by spaghetti and fettucine dishes. We once overhead two young Italian girls enthusing about a Chinese meal one had enjoyed -

"What did you eat?" one asked. "A spicy soup made with prawns, chicken and little bits of pasta," "Oooh". "Then a sweet and sour rice with vegetables and pork" "Ooh, and then?" "Then we finished with Tiramisu." "Wonderful" was the reply. Tiramisu is the well known Italian dessert of sponge, liqueur, eggs, mascarpone, coffee and chocolate served in nearly every Italian restaurant, claimed by almost every region as its own tradition, and made at home for special occasions.

The two most powerful "foodie" organisations in Italy are the Accademia Italiana della Cucina and the Arcigola Slow Food. Both are devoted to retaining the integrity of traditional Italian dishes and only support those who stick to the tried and true recipes. They also take a keen interest in the quality of wine and olive oil and are determined to see that DOC and DOCG remain marks of superior products.

All Italians take a deep proprietorial interest in the food served in their own homes and will fight to the death to convince one another that the wine, oil, rice, pasta, porchetta, etc. from their particular village is much better than, and quite unlike that, of any other village. We have sat through arguments that rumble on for some hours over this matter. Men, women, even children, take up the banner and consider no minuscule detail too small if it makes their claim more insistent.

So what do most Italians eat in a normal day and what has this to do with olive oil?

Well, the day begins with the "prima collazione" (breakfast) which is coffee and milk and a piece of bread and jam or a light pastry with a dollop of jam within it. This can be taken at home or in the nearest bar. At various intervals of the day many Italians call at their local bar for an "espresso" - that thimbleful of strong often sweet coffee that gives them a boost and can be "corrected" with grappa or some other spirit to become "caffe corretto". Many Italians finish off every meal with an "espresso" - they claim it helps them digest the food. We think it gives them the energy to get up from the table and proceed with the next ritual of the day - often an afternoon sleep! No oil, but from then on . . . .

At midday they take "pranzo" - lunch. The first course is a bowl of pasta dressed with olive oil with a tomato sauce added (not a lot, the oil must be dominant) and a little cheese sprinkled on top. Often more oil is added to this. This is followed by a thin slice of veal, coated in fine bread crumbs and lightly fried in olive oil. This is accompanied by a green vegetable (broccoli, spinach, beans, artichokes, fennel) cooked gently with a little garlic and salt in olive oil, and perhaps a dish of potatoes, gently cooked in olive oil until golden with a little garlic, rosemary, oregano or basil and salt added for flavor. Olive oil is often added at the table. This is accompanied by bread made with flour, olive oil and salt. A salad follows of green leaves (the mixture depends on the season) dressed with a little vinegar and olive oil. Fresh fruit is the final dish and an espresso coffee clears the palate. Wine is not always served, but when it is it is usually homemade or "sfuso" - fresh. Water is taken by all.

In the evening they take "cena" (dinner) This is a lighter meal if taken at home and usually consists of a bowl of soup made with olive oil, the heel of a parmigiana cheese or the leftovers from the haunch of prosciutto, vegetables, herbs and beans or chick peas, and is served accompanied by grated cheese on top and olive oil to pour in generously. Often in summer a dish of tomatoes, mozzarella cheese, and basil leaves, dressed with olive oil is served. Tomatoes, with a little salt, are always soaked in olive oil. The acid of the tomatoes and the spice of the oil do something magic together. Or supper may be a plate of bruschetta with generous olive oil, garlic and salt to which sometimes may be added fresh or pickled mushrooms, truffle paste, chicken liver paste, or just slices of fresh cheese over which is poured a little more oil. In winter supper is often a plate of beans cooked gently in olive oil with herbs, a little tomato, onion and garlic, a soffrito of carrot, parsley and celery for taste.

Fish is always best when olive oil is part of the dish and even frozen prawns gain new life and taste when olive oil is drizzled on them as they are grilled over hot coals. The "fish salad" that is so popular here for antipasto is a collection of preserved squid, little prawns, bits of fish and a few olives all marinated in olive oil to which has been added salt and a little chili. Tuna preserved in olive oil and then mixed with olive oil, salt, capers, basil or parsley, a little onion, garlic, salt and pepper is delicious.

Other uses for olive oil

Olive oil goes into cakes, biscuits, in and onto pizze, and it is good for the hair, the skin and for oiling tables and floors and wooden dishes and utensils.

Olive oil is used to preserve vegetables, and bottles of oil have chili, herbs and spices added to provide interesting flavors to salads and stews.

Olive oil is brushed on vegetables before grilling, on all meat before grilling, and is the base for salad dressings and of course, mayonnaise.

Olive oil and a little lemon juice added to pulped dried tomatoes, olives, scorched pepperoni (capsicums), cooked carrot, steamed aubergine, mashed potato for example and spiced up with a bit of cumin, salt and pepper and perhaps chili makes wonderful pastes for spreading on crostini, or sauces to have with meat or fish. Choose your ingredients and add handfuls of herbs and whizz the whole lot up in a food processor. They keep for weeks in the fridge but are usually eaten well before then.

We could go on for hours, but you get the picture. Without olive oil Italian cooking is dead.

Here are a few representative dishes that rely for their taste and integrity on olive oil.

Pizza with potato and rosemary

Make a dough with 500 gm. plain flour, a dessert spoon of salt, about four tablespoons of oil and I dessert spoon of instant yeast started in 250 ml. of warm water, a teaspoon of sugar, and a tablespoon of flour sprinkled on top. Add more water to the dough until it is soft and pliable. Leave to rise for about an hour in a covered dish in a warm place.

Thinly slice two large potatoes or four medium sized ones. Put them in a bowl and add several cloves of garlic crushed and chopped, a good handful of fresh rosemary leaves chopped finely, a little lemon zest cut very fine, a good sprinkle of salt and then about 3 tablespoons of olive oil.
Mix this up with your hands so that all the potato is covered in oil and herbs.

When the dough has risen, take it out and roll it out as thinly as you wish - for a crisp dough this will have to be very thin. It should be no more than a centimetre thick if you want to enjoy the potato taste above all. Stretch the dough to fill a flat tray, place the potato on top making sure all the surface is covered and put aside for about half an hour just to rise a bit more.

Put into a hot oven (we use 225°C with fan) for about 20 minutes. When the potato has crisped a bit, take it out and eat hot or cold.

Focaccia

The same dough can be bulked up and used to make focaccia in the following manner. Use a pie dish or a 25 cm. diameter cake tin. After the first rising, roll the dough out or stretch it into the tin. It should be about 2 cm or more high. Make holes with your finger in the dough and sprinkle over the top some oregano, or mint, or rosemary, or pieces of olives, or pieces of dried tomatoes, or bits of finely sliced onion, or onion or cumin seed, and pour oil over the top so that the holes fill. Sprinkle salt over the top and let rise until doubled again.

Put in a hot oven for about 25 minutes - we use 250°C with fan for 10 minutes and then 200° C without fan for about another 20 minutes.

Here are two pasta sauces which rely on oil as their main ingredient.

Sage and pasta

Cook fettucine (500 gm. for four people) in ample well salted boiling water. In a frying pan heat up about 6 tablespoons of olive oil. Add a dozen or so leaves of fresh sage and just let them heat through. Take off the heat, drain the pasta and put it in a bowl, pour the sage and oil over the fettucine and add a little butter and a bit of water from the pasta to make sure the fettucine is well coated. Serve with grated cheese for those who like it.

Chilli and pasta

Cook about 500 gms. of spaghetti in a saucepan of ample well salted boiling water. In a frying pan heat 6 tablespoons of olive oil. Add some dry flaked chili and about four cloves of finely chopped garlic. Drain the pasta, and coat with the hot chili and garlic oil. Have grated cheese handy for those who like it and a dish of basil leaves to add to the pasta for a pleasant addition.

Grilled vegetables

In summer most of us have an outside grill in daily use or we use a griddle over a gas flame to cook our vegetables.

We use zucchini sliced lengthwise, or aubergine, or potatoes, or capsicums.

The vegetables are sliced then brushed quite heavily with oil, sprinkled with salt and garlic and herbs and left to absorb this before being put on a medium grill or griddle. In the case of aubergine, they should be sprinkled with salt and left for an hour or so to reduce the water content, then rinsed and dried before the oil is put on. Don't cook oiled vegetables on high heat as this will scorch the outside and not cook the inside and the result with be tough and unpleasant. What you want to achieve is a soft centre and a nice smoky exterior. After the vegetables are cooked they are put on a flat plate and more oil is poured over them, perhaps add a dash of lemon juice and a few fresh herbs - in summer, whole leaves of basil. You can put mozzarella cheese on top and grill the vegetables and cheese for a few minutes in an oven, or just sprinkle grated Parmesan cheese on the top before serving. Or a fresh tomato sauce can be lightly added, or a green sauce made with fresh herbs and olive oil and perhaps a little lemon juice.

Steamed vegetables with oil

An alternative (specially for green vegetables such as spinach, broccoli, green beans and asparagus) is to steam the vegetables for about five minutes to lightly cook them. Don't refresh them but put them straight into a shallow dish in which you have already mixed up a good quantity of olive oil, the juice of half a lemon or a teaspoon of balsamic vinegar, a little crushed garlic, a touch of chili, salt and pepper. Mix thoroughly, add herbs if you wish, and leave for a couple of hours. Serve at a tepid temperature.

Veal slices in oil

Have the butcher cut very thin slices of veal. Soak them in a beaten egg and crushed garlic, salt and pepper and juice of half a lemon. Or soak them in milk to which has been added garlic, herbs, salt and pepper.

When ready to cook heat 2 table spoons of olive oil in a pan. Dip the veal in fine bread crumbs and put into the hot oil. Cook only for half a minute on each side and then leave for a few minutes on a flat plate to rest.

These are usually served as they are with a slice of lemon. If you wish you can serve them with an oil rich tomato sauce, or mushrooms cooked in oil with herbs and then add a little cream to make a smooth sauce, or even an avgolimone sauce. This is a cup of stock heated and then taken off the stove and poured over a generous amount of lemon juice (say the juice of one large or two small lemons) beaten with a couple of egg yolks. Whisk as you pour or the whole thing will curdle. Reheat very gently until the sauce thickens but be careful as it will curdle if boiled. Add a handful of chopped loveage, parsley, some basil or even a little chopped mint, check for seasoning and either serve separately or pour over the veal.

Mashed potatoes

A favorite to serve with this veal is mashed potatoes. Peel and boil enough potatoes for your family. When they are soft take from the fire, strain, and mash with plenty of olive oil, crushed and chopped garlic, a handful of chopped herbs (basil or lovage are particularly good), salt and pepper until the mixture is smooth and creamy. Check for taste, pile into a bowl, drizzle on a little olive oil, add a sprig of herbs and serve.

A winter casserole

This is left to cook gently in an oven or on top of the stove or at the side of the fireplace. It can be made from pork, chicken, rabbit or beef.

Slice several onions and gently soften in a good quantity of olive oil. Add a diced carrot, a diced stick of celery, some chopped parsley and some finely diced lemon zest. Then add some cloves of garlic finely diced or whole as you wish. When the flavors begin to rise add your meat chopped into good bite sized pieces and brown a little. Add a cup of red wine and some juniper berries, a little orange zest and juice, perhaps some fennel seed, salt and pepper. Add a small bouquet of sage, thyme, a bay leaf and rosemary tied together with string. Cover with water, add a sprinkle of salt and some black pepper and bring to the boil. Cover tightly - we put a piece of greaseproof paper over the meat and then a good heavy lid on top of the saucepan, some people put a bit of dough around the edge of the pot to seal it. Let it simmer for at least four hours. Then remove the herbs and check that the sauce is nice and smooth. If it is still a bit thin, remove the meat, and render the sauce down a bit, or if you haven't got time for that add a teaspoon or so of cornflour and let it boil for a few minutes to thicken it. Return the meat to the pot and serve.

A cake made with olive oil

We don't eat many fried sweets, but there are many that are made of various types of dough and fried in olive oil for taste.

However, we do help friends pick their grapes and we usually take with us an Italian cake that is a traditional vendemmia treat.

Usually it is made with Italian grapes - malvasia that are sweet and very good, but we have a vine brought over here from Cobdogla in South Australia and the sultanas it produces are particularly suitable for this cake as they are both delicate and well perfumed and, best of all, have a thin skin that provides a better texture than the thicker skinned Italian varieties. This recipe has come through many hands, but here is our version:

2 large eggs, 150 gm. sugar, 4 tablespoons of olive oil, 60 gm. butter (unsalted if possible), 5 tablespoons milk, some vanilla flavoring, 200 gm. plain flour and a teaspoon of baking powder, the grated zest of a lemon and the grated zest of an orange, a dash of nutmeg and a little demerara sugar. Two cups of fresh sultana grapes taken from the stem. A 23 cm springform cake tin.

Beat the eggs and sugar until pale lemon and thick. Add oil, butter and milk and the vanilla. Stir in the flour sifted with the baking powder to which you have added the two zests and the nutmeg. Stir just over a cup of the sultanas into the batter and spoon it all into the buttered and floured cake tin. Bake for about 15 minutes at 180°C and then take out, sprinkle the rest of the grapes over the top of the cake and sprinkle a little demerara sugar over them. Replace in the over and leave for another 40 minutes. Allow to cool and then just before serving shake some icing sugar over the top and place on a plate on which you have put a base of green grape leaves.

The end of the discovery trail

We began our eating lives in Australia using dripping for roast dinners, and salted butter on our bread and in our cakes. Over time we replaced the dripping with vegetable oil and the butter with margarine. A little later we replaced margarine with unsalted butter, which was not easy to find in Australia, and began to use olive oil for cooking. We used ghee for Indian food.

When we moved to Italy we found that unsalted butter was the norm and salted butter was not available. We could not find ghee. We could easily buy lard but by then the advertisers had convinced us that animal fat was dangerous and so we didn't pursue that path. However, now that we buy extremely light and fine puff pastry made with lard and find it a great improvement on the butter based pastry, we are looking at it with new eyes. We nearly gave up vegetable oil and started to use olive oil for flavor as well as something to cook in.

Now we use vegetable oil to fry in. We use unsalted butter for Indian food. We are about to use lard in pastry. And we use olive oil for all the things that Italian families do. The taste has become essential to our table.

Our family - still living in Australia and New Zealand - are just as keen on olive oil as we are.

Those in New Zealand now have their own olive trees and are, this year, preserving their own olives from those trees. There are not enough olives yet for oil, but when there are they will have them pressed. When visiting us, they put on the table, as a matter of course, a jug of our olive oil and dress their vegetables, soups and bread with it.

In Australia our daughter is having her second year of her own olive oil. Finding mature olive trees in her new garden, she quickly got on the trail of some Italian neighbors who are delighted to have some extra trees to pick and who take the olives to a local mill and share out the oil - half for them, half for our daughter.

We find that the best appreciated gift we can take to friends is a bottle of our olive oil and we often send overseas visitors home clutching bottles, strongly sealed to prevent leakages in the aeroplane taking them home. In Italy, we have discovered, oil is better than chocolates and even better than wine. Long may it continue thus.

INDEX